The 1960s

EXAMINING POP CULTURE

DAVID M. HAUGEN AND MATTHEW J. BOX,
Book Editors

Bruce Glassman, Vice President

Bonnie Szumski, Publisher

Helen Cothran, Managing Editor

GREENHAVEN PRESS
An imprint of Thomson Gale, a part of The Thomson Corporation

THOMSON

GALE

Detroit • New York • San Francisco • San Diego • New Haven, Conn.
Waterville, Maine • London • Munich

LIBRARY OF CONGRESS CATALOGING-IN-PUBLICATION DATA

The 1960s / David M. Haugen and Matthew J. Box, book editors.
    p. cm.—(Examining pop culture)
Includes bibliographical references and index.
ISBN 0-7377-2561-3 (lib. : alk. paper)
    1. Popular culture—United States—History—20th century. 2. United States—Social life and customs—1945–1970. I. Haugen, David M., 1969– . II. Box, Matthew J., 1976– . III. Series.
E169.02.A145 2005
973.923—dc22   2004060636

CONTENTS

rious experimental films of the 1960s utilized documentary realism to examine the counterculture and record social change.

Chapter 3: Music and the Counterculture

Chapter 4: The Influence of the 1960s on Post-60s Pop Culture

FOREWORD

POPULAR CULTURE IS THE COMMON SET OF ARTS, entertainments, customs, beliefs, and values shared by large segments of society. Russel B. Nye, one of the founders of the study of popular culture, wrote that "not until the appearance of mass society in the eighteenth century could popular culture, as one now uses the term, be said to exist." According to Nye, the Industrial Revolution and the rise of democracy in the eighteenth and nineteenth centuries led to increased urbanization and the emergence of a powerful middle class. In nineteenth-century Europe and North America, these trends created audiences for the popular arts that were larger, more concentrated, and more well off than at any point in history. As a result, more people shared a common culture than ever before.

The technological advancements of the twentieth century vastly accelerated the spread of popular culture. With each new advance in mass communication—motion pictures, radio, television, and the Internet—popular culture has become an increasingly pervasive aspect of everyday life.

Popular entertainment—in the form of movies, television, theater, music recordings and concerts, books, magazines, sporting events, video games, restaurants, casinos, theme parks, and other attractions—is one very recognizable aspect of popular culture. In his 1999 book *The Entertainment Economy: How Mega-Media Forces Are Transforming Our Lives*, Michael J. Wolf argues that entertainment is becoming the dominant feature of American society: "In choosing where we buy French fries, how we relate to political candidates, what airline we want to fly, what pajamas we choose for our kids, and which mall we want to buy them in, entertainment is increasingly influencing every one of those choices. . . . Multiply that by the billions of choices that, collectively, all of us make each day and you have a portrait of a society in which entertainment is one of its leading institutions."

It is partly this pervasive quality of popular culture that makes it worthy of study. James Combs, the author of *Polpop: Politics and Popular Culture in America*, explains that examining

7

popular culture is important because it can shape people's attitudes and beliefs:

> Popular culture is so much a part of our lives that we cannot deny its developmental powers. . . . Like formal education or family rearing, popular culture is part of our "learning environment.". . . Though our pop culture education is informal—we usually do not attend to pop culture for its "educational" value—it nevertheless provides us with information and images upon which we develop our opinions and attitudes. We would not be what we are, nor would our society be quite the same, without the impact of popular culture.

Examining popular culture is also important because popular movies, music, fads, and the like often reflect popular opinions and attitudes. Christopher D. Geist and Jack Nachbar explain in *The Popular Culture Reader*, "the popular arts provide a gauge by which we can learn what Americans are thinking, their fears, fantasies, dreams, and dominant mythologies. The popular arts reflect the values of the multitude."

This two-way relationship between popular culture and society is evident in many modern discussions of popular culture. Does the glorification of guns by many rap artists, for example, merely reflect the realities of inner-city life, or does it also contribute to the problem of gun violence? Such questions also arise in discussions of the popular culture of the past. Did the Vietnam protest music of the late 1960s and early 1970s, for instance, simply reflect popular antiwar sentiments, or did it help turn public opinion against the war? Examining such questions is an important part of understanding history.

Greenhaven Press's *Examining Pop Culture* series provides students with the resources to begin exploring these questions. Each volume in the series focuses on a particular aspect of popular culture, with topics as varied as popular culture itself. Books in the series may focus on a particular genre, such as *Rap and Hip Hop*, while others may cover a specific medium, such as *Computers and the Internet*. Volumes such as *Body Piercing and Tattoos* have their focus on recent trends in popular culture, while titles like *Americans' Views About War* have a broader historical scope.

In each volume, an introductory essay provides a general

overview of the topic. The selections that follow offer a survey of critical thought about the subject. The readings in *Americans' Views About War*, for example, are arranged chronologically: Essays explore how popular films, songs, television programs, and even comic books both reflected and shaped public opinion about American wars from World War I through Vietnam. The essays in *Violence in Film and Television*, on the other hand, take a more varied approach: Some provide historical background, while others examine specific genres of violent film, such as horror, and still others discuss the current controversy surrounding the issue.

Each book in the series contains a comprehensive index to help readers quickly locate material of interest. Perhaps most importantly, each volume has an annotated bibliography to aid interested students in conducting further research on the topic. In today's culture, what is "popular" changes rapidly from year to year and even month to month. Those who study popular culture must constantly struggle to keep up. The volumes in Greenhaven's *Examining Pop Culture* series are intended to introduce readers to the major themes and issues associated with each topic, so they can begin examining for themselves what impact popular culture has on their own lives.

The Personal and Political in 1960s' Pop Culture

AMERICAN POP CULTURE IS OFTEN PORTRAYED AS a set of customs and rituals, attitudes and behaviors, trends and tastes, that establish unity among members of a society. Outside of this definition lies the divisive world of politics and social agendas—matters that have a sense of social imperative, a gravity that separates them from the idle pursuits that typically clutter up the pop culture scene. In the decade of the 1960s, however, the dividing line between the serious and the slight, the momentous and the mundane, was not so obvious. The culture of the 1960s was dominated by unprecedented political and social turmoil and change, and perhaps unlike any other period in American history, pop culture of the decade reflected the upheaval. "The personal became political," Alexander Bloom writes, "and the cultural and political seemed to be two parts of a whole."[1] Everyday activities—from putting on clothes to choosing music to reading a book—carried a message: One was either part of the change, or one was against it. Many leisurely distractions therefore explicitly or subtly betrayed an affiliation with more serious concerns of the day, even as they may have proffered a way to escape those concerns.

The Youthful Decade

Pop culture of the 1960s was driven by change. The major impetus behind that change was the baby boom generation that had been born in the years just after World War II. In the 1960s many of these young people came of age. In fact, by the end of the decade around 36 million Americans were between fifteen and twenty-four years old. The political, creative, and

economic power of this section of the national population en-
sured that the focus of the decade was on youth.

The results of the 1960 presidential election seemed to
herald this cultural swell. The victor, John F. Kennedy, was the
youngest president yet to serve. Kennedy's predecessor was the
famed World War II general Dwight D. Eisenhower, a president who ruled over—and even represented—the complacent
and conservative America of the 1950s. Kennedy's agenda as
chief executive aimed at capitalizing on the youthful vigor that
lay dormant at the end of Eisenhower's reign. In his inaugural
address, Kennedy acknowledged that the Cold War era had set
America against ideological rivals, but he insisted that the common enemies were "tyranny, poverty, disease, and war itself."[2]
He called upon the young to serve their country and humanity.
And since racism, poverty, and injustice were rampant in the
United States, many young people were given excuses to use
their newfound public spirit to shape a better America. The resulting youth movement, therefore, began to define itself by
how much it could correct the problems of the previous generations, and in doing so many young people came to believe that
the elders who were still in charge of the nation might not possess the most altruistic vision of democracy.

The Counterculture

As a result of the perceived conflict of interest, many of America's young people reacted against anything that smacked of
the establishment—the rooted power of the "over thirty" generations that, by a popular aphorism, were not to be trusted. In
the early 1960s the rebellion began on college campuses where
mostly white, voting-age students examined the nation's policies toward integration, civil rights, and growing involvement
in a war in Southeast Asia. By mid-decade, the students had
organized and participated in voter registration drives for
black voters in the South and staged protests against further
military buildup in Vietnam. Kennedy's push for activism had
come back to bite the United States on the heel, but Kennedy
had not lived to see it. The symbol of youth was assassinated
in 1963, leaving his followers disheartened but also leaderless.
"The movement"—as the political arm of the youth uprising
was collectively called—no longer had the chief of state as its

guide; so the young banded together to fight the establishment on their own terms.

When the movement took to the streets in the mid-1960s to protest against Vietnam, it began to pull in other elements from the population at large. After all, any male who had just reached adulthood—regardless of education—could be drafted to serve in the war. Young men of all backgrounds gravitated to the movement. Some had moral or philosophic objections to the war; others simply did not want to die. Women also streamed into the movement. Among them, the wives and lovers of service-age men, as well as others who were finding out that the movement offered a taste of political action which, for women, had been largely ignored in previous generations. In addition, the championing of civil rights also helped bring the white and black youth into closer union.

The movement, then, began to foment its own culture that stood in opposition not only to the Vietnam War and political injustice, but also to the values in mainstream American society that activists blamed for these problems and all the evils that beset the nation. As British historian Arthur Marwick states, the term "counterculture" ultimately referred to "the many and varied activities and values which contrasted with, or were critical of, the conventional values and modes of established society."[3] With factions and subgroups embracing so many disparate causes, though, this counterculture was amorphous and had no central logic other than its antithetical association with the mainstream.

Music, Politics, and Money

Even without a central doctrine, the counterculture still had defining elements, many of which have been handed down as pop culture legacies. Chief among these was the music of the new generation. While rock and roll had already divided young and old in the 1950s, during the 1960s the rift was widened. Rock and roll of the 1950s may have been an expression of rebellion, but it lacked the political drive of the new decade's music. Sixties' rock inherited its social conscience from the resurgence of folk music in New York City's East Village in the first three years of the decade. Troubadours such as Bob Dylan, Phil Ochs, and Joan Baez studied and played the works of folk masters from the 1930s—another period in American history when music was tightly bound up with social change. Dylan, Ochs, Baez, and others learned the unifying and persuasive power of folk music and began writing their own songs to relate to new national crises. Dylan's "A Hard Rain's a-Gonna Fall," for example, spoke of the impending threat of nuclear war that hung over the nation during the Cuban missile crisis in 1962. Such songs helped create a folk scene in New York that eventually crossed over into the mainstream when less grubby and less militant performers such as Peter, Paul, and Mary began making regular television appearances.

The co-opting of the folk scene, however, did not spell its doom. Rather, it was the advent of Beatlemania in America that pushed folk and all other music out of the pop culture spotlight. When the Beatles first crossed the Atlantic in 1964, the furor of their reception was headline news. The four British bandmates had a blues-based style, a clean-cut look, and a collective wit and charm that won over America's youth. The nation's adults merely tolerated them, sometimes noting that their mop-top hairdos were too shaggy by respectable standards. Beatlemania, though, went beyond love or contempt for the band or its music; Beatlemania was about marketing a phenomenon. As Beatle fan and biographer Nicholas Schaffner writes, "Only a fraction of the boom Beatle industry had anything to do with music. The real action was Beatle merchandise. . . . There were Beatle brands of just about every sort of junk food, knick-knack, stationery, toy, clothing, and jewelry; one could put a touch of Beatles into almost every conceivable aspect of one's life."[4] American capitalism cashed in on the Beatles craze, grossing over $50 million in product sales in the first year of their visit. Although the Beatles were not the first fad to be heavily merchandised, they were the first music group to have made such a cultural and economic impact.

The Drug Culture

As the Beatles themselves tired of worldwide Beatlemania, they left behind the infectious but innocent songs of their early career and said good-bye to touring in 1966. They began listening to the collective voice of the counterculture as it spread from America to England. Mimicking the young people's cry for peace and unity, the Beatles started writing more socially conscious songs and focused on creating more cohesive albums that would appeal to discerning listeners. On their 1966 record *Revolver*, they even dabbled with a new musical style that was coming out of San Francisco at the time. The psychedelic sound, or acid rock—as this new music was dubbed—was an attempt to capture the supposedly mind-expanding experience one had while under the influence of psychedelic drugs such as LSD. Though the Beatles had not pioneered this music, which coupled wild lyrical imagery with a propulsive beat, their exploration of this creative outlet showed how influential the American counterculture was.

San Francisco's psychedelic scene was born in the Haight-Ashbury district of the city. In the early-to-mid-1960s the neighborhood was a haven for counterculture poets, artists, musicians, and social activists. The liberal, artistic climate allowed for much experimentation. Activists opened free stores where donated items were given away to those in need; idealists tried their hand at communal living; and nearly everyone had some experience with the burgeoning drug culture. The new drug of choice for this scene was lysergic acid diethylamide (LSD), or "acid" for short. Introduced to the Bay Area in 1965, LSD became the focal point of several "acid tests" in which San Francisco's youth would congregate at a predetermined location, take a hit of the new drug, and then dance to the droning beats of local bands like the Warlocks (the group that would later rename themselves the Grateful Dead).

LSD was still legal in 1965, so the acid tests were not an outlaw manifestation of youth rebellion. In fact, the chief guru and promoter of acid was Timothy Leary, a former Harvard professor who believed the drug offered a means of self-discovery and a new form of perception since, according to Leary, it tapped into the large percentage of the human brain that goes unused in daily life. Acid among the youth culture was not a tool of resistance; it was a path of escape. Still, it was an escape from the bland conformity of the middle class, the supposed limitations of institutional education, and the national predilections for war and consumerism. The *counter*culture, therefore, did not insist on *countering* the mainstream through militant protest; one could show allegiance to the counterculture by rejecting the values of mainstream America while trying to forge new realities where new paradigms held sway.

Hippies: Alternative Culture Becomes Pop Culture

The segment of the counterculture most associated with the rejection of mainstream values in the 1960s was the hippie movement. Hippies were a product of the Haight-Ashbury environment. Although they could and did rally to political causes, the hippies were theoretically nonmilitant. They proffered peace and love as alternatives to the violence and racism that seemed to engulf America at the time. They discarded America's mores and embraced its taboos. Hippies grew their hair long, and they wore wild and colorful clothing that stood in stark contrast to the conservative styles of the day. They indulged in sexual liberation and free love, since they typically believed marriage was too confining. They took to sharing and communal living as a remedy to the nation's consumer culture. And they defied racism by adopting a notion of general brotherhood that drew all ethnicities into the fold. Indeed, the personal had become political.

The hippie movement spread throughout the country in the late 1960s (and beyond). Those who did not have the means to travel to San Francisco to be in the mecca of hippie culture still had the music of that scene to inspire them. And because aspiring to hippie ideals did not require anything other than a change in ethical and perhaps aesthetic views, millions of young people in America's white suburbs—the bastion of conservatism—could dabble in the music, the dress, and even the philosophical tenets of the counterculture without giving up the security and comfort of mainstream life. Once the trends spread to large sections of the affluent, mainstream children, however, hippiedom could not be ignored. Instead, as with Beatlemania, it was marketed. Chic clothing stores began selling bright paisley fashions, and manufactured rock groups began churning out songs that tried to capture the essence of peace and love without a sense of genuine commitment. Hippieness had finally been subsumed by mainstream pop culture, but the essential message was not entirely lost in the process. Pressured by nagging questions over the righteousness of fighting a war in Vietnam, the paradoxical notion of depriving certain people of their civil rights in a democracy, and the possibility that pleasure may exist outside of economic well-being, American mainstream culture became more liberalized. The protest movement was certainly influential in pointing out and confronting injustices, but the hippies were equally important in causing the culture shift. As author and former hippie Barry Miles explains: "It was only by stepping outside society that people were able to look at it objectively—to see what was wrong with it, to see how they'd like to change it."[5] And the hippies showed America how that could be done.

Celluloid Mirrors

Another group that offered Americans a view of themselves and the world that they had made were the filmmakers of the 1960s. At the beginning of the decade, Hollywood studios were on the verge of bankruptcy. Television—the new entertainment gadget—had obviated many people's need to go out to the movies. Hollywood tried to carry on with its age-old formulas until it learned a lesson from the new independent studios that cropped up to fill the needs of those bored by big-studio fare. Unable to finance big-budget extravaganzas that would play only to half-filled theaters, independent film studios began producing low-budget films with unknown talent and untested directors. The combination of these new creative forces, however, would have a tremendous impact on Hollywood and on American filmmaking itself.

Roger Corman, the maverick producer-director of American International Pictures, was perhaps the poster child for shoestring productions. His films were usually successful moneymakers for the nation's drive-in circuit because Corman had his pulse on the times. His work ranged from horror films to comedies to action movies, but each film was targeted at a singular audience—young people. Films like *The Wild Angels* (1966), about free-spirited, yet potentially violent bikers, and *The Trip* (1967), about the drug culture in Haight-Ashbury, capitalized on the rebellious or outlaw spirit of the counterculture. In these pictures Corman was able to mirror the youth culture back on itself and with an immediacy that was spawned out of the demands of working with paltry finances and tight shooting dates. His best films also were never schmaltzy; they portrayed their young protagonists as individuals in search of some moral ground amidst the chaos and confusion of 1960s society.

Other directors—some working within Hollywood, some outside of it—also attuned their pictures to the temper of the times. Dennis Hopper's four-hundred-thousand-dollar road epic *Easy Rider* (1969) depicts two young free spirits motorcycling through America's byways. Although their journey has something to do with a drug deal (from which they ostensibly finance their life on the road), it is quickly apparent that the travels of Billy and Wyatt reflect the counterculture's desire to live outside the mainstream, in a world where freedom is equated with the open road. By movie's end, however, Billy's and Wyatt's escape culminates in a tragedy, as both are shot down wantonly by rednecks who represent the mainstream in their disapproval of Billy's and Wyatt's counterculture appearance. The death of the protagonists, therefore, stands as the prophetic death of the counterculture—the flawed idea that freedom lies in mythologizing America's open spaces as an alternative to being trapped in mainstream society. But the movie is not entirely sour in its outlook. Billy and Wyatt became cult heroes to the 1960s generation because they lived out their ideals, even in the face of the forces that would ultimately crush them. "We knew there couldn't be any more heroes," Peter Fonda, who portrayed Wyatt, stated in an interview, "yet we still tried to *live* like heroes. This yearning is there in the film—along with the disillusionment."[6]

While *Easy Rider, The Trip,* and other films tried to connect with the counterculture, other movies contended with other concerns of the day. John Frankenheimer's *The Manchurian Candidate* (1962) focuses on Cold War politics and eerily foreshadowed the assassination of President Kennedy. Robert Mulligan's film version of *To Kill a Mockingbird* (1962) foregrounds racial injustice. And Stanley Kubrick's *Dr. Strangelove* (1963) paints a morbidly comic vision of how close America was to nuclear conflict. Like many of the films of the decade, each of these pictures served both as entertainment and as social commentary. *The Manchurian Candidate,* for example, is a deft political thriller involving the U.S. military, but it also forces viewers to see that the patriotism embodied in America's soldiers might be undercut by the fact that soldiers—and by extension, any government officials—are in the words of critic Steffen Haubner, "unsuspecting pawns . . . [and] political sheep following invisible herders and meaningless ideologies."[7] The thematic tensions of Frankenheimer's film are, therefore, reinforced by the social criticism of the era in which blind obedience was questioned and ideologies were reevaluated. But the criticism is not only aimed at the establishment. All ideologies are portrayed as corrupt; the counterculture was made up of just as many sheep as mainstream America. Therein lies the paradox of the film and the decade. Broadening this contradictory viewpoint to other films of the 1960s and beyond, critic Jürgen Müller asserts, "The movies of the decade reflect its inherent contradictions, and humanity is still suffering from the failure to overcome them."[8]

Television and the Conspicuous Absence

While some films of the 1960s did engage with the changing social and political climate of the nation, Hollywood continued to produce big-budget spectacles like *Cleopatra* (1963) that were pure escapist fare. But the true medium of escape in the 1960s was television. The most popular broadcast programs of the decade were Westerns, variety shows, comedies, and police or spy dramas. None of these shows dared to comment on the world around them; in fact, most played it safe by hiding behind the constraints of their genre. Westerns created a fictional world where good and evil were black and white. Variety shows, such as *The Ed Sullivan Show*, were unapologetically conservative and attempted to be apolitical in an effort to cater to a wide audience. Comedies, for the most part, ranged from the fantastical, such as *Bewitched*, in which the fantasy element took center stage, to *The Beverly Hillbillies*, in which the clash of cultures (sophisticated urbanites and unvarnished hill folk) reflected a moral, not a political, disparity. Finally, the detective dramas of the era sometimes dealt with Cold War espionage but always in a facile manner that kept the comic book world of "us and them" undisturbed. Even as the decade wore on and social protest erupted into violence outside the Democratic convention in Chicago in 1968, television programming remained in its own world. As cultural critic Josh Ozersky attests, "Few things are more striking, in retrospect, than the sheer obliviousness of prime-time television in 1968 to the turmoil surrounding it in the real world."[9]

Television's connection to the political and social change of the 1960s, therefore, was the conspicuous absence of timely programming. Prime-time fare provided the perfect escape from the gravity of the decade, and that was all entertainment programming was expected to do. Nightly news shows brought the events of the day into America's homes. Images of southern policemen turning dogs and fire hoses on civil rights protesters, students shouting out against the establishment, black rioters in urban ghettos, and soldiers holding on in Vietnam (along with daily death tolls from that war) made Americans highly aware of (if not completely informed about) the subjects that were dividing the nation. Prime-time broadcasts, in some ways, tried to subvert the troublesome images of the nightly news. While news reports of soldiers in Vietnam suggested fear and aggression, *Gomer Pyle, U.S.M.C.* offered a happy-go-lucky version of the military in which high jinks prevailed over soldierly duties. And if the news examined racist politics in the South, the networks countered with likable and harmless country bumpkins in *The Beverly Hillbillies* and *Hee Haw.*

By the late 1960s some prime-time fare did challenge the status quo. *The Smothers Brothers Comedy Hour* and *Laugh-In* were two variety shows that targeted the youth culture as an audience. The former, as Josh Ozersky writes, "appealed to the young without alienating their parents or grandparents."[10] Tom and Dick Smothers were a pair of comedians and folk singers who dressed very conservatively. Their comedy was very tame by today's standards, but it was also thoughtful and often delved into the language and issues of the counterculture. As the show progressed from its debut in 1967, the two brothers' leftist leanings got the better of them. They antagonized the CBS network by infusing more politics into their sketches and their choice of guests (one of whom, folk singer Pete Seeger, had been blacklisted from the media since 1950 for his pro-labor, antiwar, and antiauthoritarian views). By 1969 the show was slated for cancellation.

Like the Smothers Brothers' show, *Laugh-In* indulged in the counterculture, but in a way that was not a confrontational assault on the mainstream. *Laugh-In*'s cast borrowed the vibrant wordplay as well as the dress of the youth culture, and the set designers incorporated the colorful imagery of the "in" crowd. Together with rapid sketch sequences and zoom in, zoom out camera work, these elements helped the show capture the immediacy and vigor of the youth movement. But the antics of this variety show were patently absurdist. They posed no threat to mainstream viewers who might not have understood the humor but were not offended by it either. Still, the nonlinear, rapid-fire sequencing of the program showed that its allegiance was to the new and innovative culture and not to the formulaic complacency of many television shows in the 1960s.

The 1960s Today

While much of 1960s' pop culture reveled in innovation and the shedding of old standards and practices, its current value seems to lie more in the realm of kitsch. The pop culture of the era has been largely stripped of its political force and infused with nostalgia. Many of those men who played with GI Joe dolls when they were children in the 1960s, for example, look back fondly on those toys today without associating them with the militaristic atmosphere of the decade. And millions of older baby boomers claim to have made the pilgrimage to the Woodstock music festival—the high-water mark of the counterculture's outpouring of peace and togetherness—when attendance estimates reach only as high as five-hundred thousand. The younger generations that grew up with the rebelliousness of the 1960s already tamed and firmly woven into the social and political framework of the nation have even less of a sense of the relevance of that era's pop culture. Today, sixties' movies that deal with the counterculture are likely singled out for their outlandish wardrobes and their passé vocabularies. Similarly, sixties' music may have a timeless social applicability, but the urgency of the message now seems lost.

Later decades' subsuming of 1960s' popular culture, however, is not something to be mourned. The spirit of the hippie culture, of the music of protest, and of the filmic visions that overturned old conventions has now become a given, and the entire culture shift that made room for counterculture ideals has become the norm. As history professor Marilyn B. Young remarks, "The rejection of the political culture of the nuclear family, corporate capitalism, and military aggression, expressed through an embrace of sex, drugs, and rock and roll, turned out not to be nearly as corrosive as antibourgeois youth thought or wished."[11] Instead, the culture shift simply became another foundational layer for succeeding generations. In the post-1960s world, Americans feel inclined to question the government; they assume music can be political and engaging; and they expect that many films will be commentaries of their times. Much of today's pop culture—indeed, today's mainstream culture—is therefore indebted to these revolutionary sixties' attitudes that were first made manifest when pop culture and political culture collided in that gone-but-not-forgotten decade.

Notes

1. Alexander Bloom, ed., *Long Time Gone: Sixties America Then and Now*. New York: Oxford University Press, 2001, p. 8.

2. John F. Kennedy, inaugural address, January 20, 1961.

3. Arthur Marwick, *The Sixties: Cultural Revolution in Britain, France, Italy, and the United States, c. 1958–c. 1974*. New York: Oxford University Press, 1998, p. 12.

4. Nicholas Schaffner, *The Beatles Forever*. Harrisburg, PA: Cameron House, 1978, p. 14.

5. Barry Miles, *Hippie*. New York: Sterling, 2004, p. 18.

6. Quoted in Jürgen Müller, ed., *Movies of the 60s*. Los Angeles: Taschen, 2004, p. 572.

7. Quoted in Müller, *Movies of the 60s*, p. 141.

8. Müller, *Movies of the 60s*, p. 17.

9. Josh Ozersky, *Archie Bunker's America: TV in an Era of Change, 1968–1978*. Carbondale: Southern Illinois University Press, 2003, p. 1.

10. Ozersky, *Archie Bunker's America*, p. 33.

11. Marilyn B. Young, foreword to Peter Braunstein and Michael William Doyle, eds., *Imagine Nation: The American Counterculture of the 1960s and '70s*. New York: Routledge, 2002, p. 1.

EXAMINING POP CULTURE

Pastimes and Preoccupations

Fads, Toys, and Hobbies Mix Politics and Play

Edward J. Rielly

In the following article, Edward J. Rielly enumerates many of the popular pastimes of the 1960s. According to Rielly, these diversions both "exhibited America's spirit of play" as well as revealed a common interest to escape the heady political and social issues of the day. Amusements such as the Super Ball and the yo-yo were simply great stress relievers for a decade under immense pressures. Yet, as Rielly contends, the social dynamics of the 1960s were so palpable that many of the toys, hobbies, and fads of the times often exhibited some relationship to the intensity of the social and political climate. For example, in a decade fueled by activism, the popularity of buttons and bumper stickers bespoke a person's desire to proclaim his or her position on drugs, communism, or the war in Vietnam. Edward J. Rielly is a professor of English at St. Joseph's College of Maine.

THE DECADE OF THE 1960s WAS A PERIOD OF WAR abroad and social upheaval at home, but there remained time for play. From the most popular of professional sports to children's toys, and through a variety of fads and hobbies that also exhibited America's spirit of play, the nation found itself at least at times able to turn away from its concern with political and social divisions to revel in pastimes long associated with a

■

lighter aspect of human nature. Yet so strong were the social dynamics of the decade that even play could gravitate toward the ideological, sometimes mirroring conflicts and preoccupations that were threatening to unravel the social fabric of the country.

The lines of demarcation among fads, games, toys, hobbies, and sports are often difficult to draw. A particular game or toy that proves briefly popular may be considered a fad; one person's hobby is another individual's serious, even professional sport; and a game that draws neighbors or friends together to play on a Saturday night may be a productive career for others. . . .

Fads and the Cultural Dichotomy

A fad, or craze, is any custom or activity that enjoys great, but temporary popularity. The 1960s included a great many fads, perhaps more than in many other decades because of the nation's general prosperity during the decade. More disposable money meant that less thought needed to be given to the long-term value of a purchase. Inclinations could be satisfied, and often were.

Most homes, for example, did not want for light, but individuals seeking maximum pleasure and profit from their moments of relaxation and meditation increasingly added a Lava Lite. Originally known as an Astrolight in Germany, where it was invented, the Lava Lite was cylindrical and contained a yellow wax heated by a coil. The Lava Lite was not bright enough to be a reading light; its purpose, instead, was to set a mood, regardless of what mood was desired. In living rooms and college rooms, the light provided visual delight as the wax took on varying forms and hues. Many people found it also a mood-setting accompaniment to whatever drugs they were taking.

The Lava Lite was not the only item that could set a mood. The water bed, invented by Charles Hall to provide something more comfortable than the then popular beanbag furniture, became instead a major sex symbol of the late 1960s. It appealed to the counterculture and to the very rich. Hugh Hefner established a king-sized model in his Chicago mansion. Water beds, however, had an unfortunate tendency in their early days to collapse floors and spring leaks that proved dangerous to the electrical heaters that kept the water warm. One story circulated about a couple making love in their water bed on their balcony, only to have the balcony collapse under the weight of the water (and perhaps their strenuous activity), crushing the lovers to death.

Individuals tripping on LSD were fond of "black lights," which could be purchased in "headshops" along with fluorescent paints and dyes. Fluorescent clothes or posters in the presence of black light bulbs created a visual counterpart to the effect of LSD. Restaurants and nightclubs installed black lights to appeal to those seeking drug (or druglike) effects. Day-Glo dyes and paints were attractive to the same individuals who favored black lights. Incandescent pigments of orange, red, and yellow would glow brightly in normal daylight, giving the visual effect the name of "Day-Glo." Posters, sides of vans, guitars, and countless other types of objects were painted in Day-Glo. Since the 1960s, Day-Glo colors have moved from the level of fad to standard issue in such everyday items as swimsuits and highlighting markers used in huge numbers by students. Colors also made their way to people's bodies during the 1960s, as body painting achieved short-lived but well-publicized exposure.

Buttons proclaiming slogans or favorite political candidates have been worn for a long time, but they achieved a level of popularity in the 1960s never enjoyed before or since. At the same time, bumper stickers became a staple of the automobile. The more serious messages on these buttons usually were antiwar or in some other way reflective of social attitudes. "Make love, not war"; "Tune in, turn on, drop out"; "Kill a Commie for Christ"; and countless other statements were intended at least to express one's opinion if not convert others. Many buttons addressed the increasingly liberal attitudes toward sex, such as "Cure virginity." Sometimes the button might address both the political and sexual: "Lay, don't slay." The most popular message on buttons was the antiwar symbol, expanded from its antinuclear origins—a somewhat abstract bomber pointed straight up. Many buttons, of course, were strictly frivolous: "Mary Poppins is a junkie."

Bumper stickers were more evenly divided between the established culture and the counterculture. Individuals, often older, expressed their opposition to the new culture while affirming traditional values: "God bless America"; or "Support your local police." As buttons have declined in popularity over the subsequent decades, bumper stickers have spread ever more widely. Following a car on a city street today, drivers can learn far more than they care to know about the lead driver's past destinations, political preferences, and attitudes toward other drivers, as well as the academic accomplishments of the driver's children. Bumper stickers may prove to be a fad, but, if so, at the beginning of the twenty-first century, they have become a long-lived one.

Serious Games and Silly Toys

The spirit of play in the United States continued unabated even as the political climate of the nation changed dramatically in the second half of the 1960s. So popular and varied were games and toys that only a sampling can be given here.

Many of the older games, such as cards and checkers, continued to be played by young and old. Poker and euchre were common across the age spectrum, with bridge usually associated with an older and more upscale crowd. College students enjoyed cribbage, and increasing numbers of students and young adults turned to chess. Considered by some to be a sport, and so categorized in the *Sports Illustrated 2000 Sports Almanac*, chess received a great boost from Bobby Fischer, the first chess player to become widely recognized in the United States. Robert James Fischer taught himself chess at the age of six and won the U.S. Junior Championship and the U.S. Championship by fifteen. He was U.S. champion every year from 1958 to 1967 with the exception of 1962. His most defining moment, though, came in the following decade, in 1972, when he defeated Russian Boris Spassky for the World Championship.

By the middle of the decade, Tarot cards, representing virtues and vices and used in fortune-telling, had become popular, in part responding to growing interest in alternative forms of spirituality. Similar impulses toward antiestablishment norms helped to popularize the Ouija board, which includes a planchette that, when touched, allegedly moves to spell out spiritualistic messages by pointing at letters on the board.

Adult board games introduced during the 1960s tended to

mirror real-life situations and/or appeal to the supposed intelligence of adults. Acquire and High Bid were stock market games. Jeopardy posed answers and required players to supply the questions. Diplomacy, invented by an MIT professor, included a board with seven European countries on it. The seven players attempted to take each other's countries with their armies and navies, or by forming alliances with other players. Bar-Spreezy included the bonus (or penalty) of having to sip a drink for each point won, although drawing "Intoxicards" permitted the player to skip a sip. A tamer but more intellectual game was Scrabble, which included small squares with letters on them and demanded creation of words; the person with the best vocabulary was most likely to prove victorious. Acting out words was the point of charades, a popular party game that called for a bit of acting ability and willingness to make a fool of oneself in public. Many hosts found it an effective ice-breaker.

A game for children of all ages, and much more than just a toy, was the slot car. Over three million Americans were playing with slot cars by mid-decade, including Robert Kennedy and CBS anchor Walter Cronkite. Universities, including several Ivy League schools, were home to slot-car teams. The small (usually two-inch) plastic car derived its name from a slot in the track on which the cars were raced. A projection under the car fit into the slot, and electricity powered the vehicles. When Ford brought out its Mustang in 1964, Aurora Plastics introduced a slot-car version. By 1967, however, the slot-car craze was heading downhill.

Games and toys are hard to separate, for children have always played games with toys. One of the most popular toys of the 1960s was the super ball. The super ball was a small, dense ball with the capacity to rebound almost the same distance as that from which it was dropped and continue bouncing much longer than other balls, about sixty seconds. Wham-O sold the ball for less than a dollar, and adults as well as children bought it in such numbers that Wham-O was producing 170,000 balls per day at the height of the craze. McGeorge Bundy, National Security Advisor to President Lyndon Johnson, purchased super balls for sixty members of his staff, apparently as much to help them reduce stress as for entertainment. Skateboarders liked to bounce a super ball while they skated down the street, and children used it while playing jacks. Wham-O also created such other classics as the Frisbee and the Hula-Hoop, both of which, introduced in the late 1950s, remained popular through the next decade. Early in the 1960s, children and adults alike found themselves caught up in another game involving some physical exertion, if only by the hand and wrist—the yo-yo craze.

Dolls Reflect Cultural Attitudes

An all-1960s grouping of toys would be heavy on dolls, with two very opposite dolls heading the list: Barbie and G.I. Joe. Mattel produced its first Barbie in 1958. Within five years, there were nine million Barbies residing in little girls' rooms and anywhere else girls happened to be. The doll received five hundred letters per week, although no record exists regarding how many she successfully answered. Barbie had expensive

A Man of Action Breaks Racial Barriers

Hasbro's GI Joe action figure appeared on store shelves in 1964. Although many in the first run of these "man of action" dolls had Caucasian features and white-skinned bodies, Hasbro executives did market an African American version at the same time. GI Joe biographer John Michlig explains how this black variant was received in a nation that was still coming to terms with the meaning of civil rights.

The race issue during the early 1960s was extremely volatile. George C. Wallace proclaimed "Segregation now, segregation tomorrow, and segregation forever!" during his 1963 inaugural address as governor of Alabama. In 1964, Atlanta restaurateur Lester G. Maddox—later elected governor—chose to close his establishment rather than comply with a federal order stating that he must serve Black customers, even going so far as to pass out pickax handles on the street outside his restaurant to persons willing to help tastes, with her clothes multiplying in numbers and styles. Some of her clothing items in the 1960s, such as a red velvet coat, cost more than the doll did (about three dollars). Keeping the doll inexpensive was a brilliant marketing strategy to hook youngsters and then induce continuing expenditures to keep Barbie in style.

So that Barbie would not feel alone, Mattel came up with pals for Barbie, the male Ken and the female Midge. Both of them also wore clothes, lots of them. Critics saw in the Barbie phenomenon a symbol of much that was wrong with the United States, including its commercialism and gender stereotyping. Many a parent, though, saw her or his objections crumble before a child's ardent longing for her own Barbie.

G.I. Joe was another popular and controversial doll, created in 1963 but seemingly out of sync with the growing antiwar sentiment of the second half of the 1960s. By 1966, G.I. Joe was in

him maintain the status quo. And in August 1965, the Watts section of Los Angeles was ravaged by race riots, claiming the lives of thirty-four persons and destroying more than two hundred businesses.

In this tumultuous environment, it's little wonder that Hasbro marketed the Black soldier (whose facial features were identical to the Caucasian GI Joe) exclusively in the northern states for the first few years of its existence. The Black soldier didn't sell well initially, even in urban retail outlets; store owners reported that Black children tended to pick the Caucasian GI Joe when presented with a choice. Fortunately, that trend faded as more and more multiethnic dolls appeared on the market. (Though a Black Barbie would not be created until 1980, Mattel introduced Barbie's Black friends Julia and Christie in 1969, and, most significantly, helped set up Black-run Shindana Toys in 1968 to produce multicultural playthings.)

John Michlig, *GI Joe: The Complete Story of America's Favorite Man of Action.* San Francisco: Chronicle Books, 1998, p. 111.

ten million homes. Sales of the doll did slide toward the end of the decade, with Dr. Benjamin Spock condemning it in his *Baby and Child Care*, and the doll's role was transformed into more of an explorer and adventurer, later resuming its overt combat persona. Hassenfeld Brothers put considerable thought into creation of their doll, creating Joe's face from a composite of twenty actual Congressional Medal of Honor winners. Like Mattel with Barbie, the manufacturer kept the price of the doll low (about four dollars), while the full range of clothes, equipment, and weapons ran to about two hundred dollars.

A popular theory behind Stanley Weston's development of G.I. Joe is that the purpose was to detach boys, enamored with Barbie's curvaceous characteristics, from their secret playing with her. Better guns than breasts, violence rather than sex, hence G.I. Joe, an American hero.

Other dolls did not approach Barbie and G.I. Joe in sustained popularity but had their moments. The Troll Doll, also known as the Dammit Doll after its inventor, Thomas Dam, became a favorite of college women in the 1960s. By the end of the decade, only Barbie was outselling the Troll Doll, two dolls that could not have been less alike. Unlike the sexy Barbie, the Troll was an ugly gnome with big ears and a wide nose, so ugly as to be cute. Not only college students favored the doll, which was supposed to bring good luck. Pilot Betty Miller had a Troll Doll co-pilot on her duplication of Amelia Earhart's 1935 flight, and Lady Bird Johnson shared the White House with her husband and one of the gnomes.

As pressure to achieve equal rights regardless of race picked up steam in the later 1960s, so did the movement make its way into the world of toys. Baby Nancy, from Shindana, appeared in time for Christmas 1968. Nancy was clearly African American in features, color, and hair, and sold for five to six dollars. The Black Doll Toy Company produced "Soul Babies" and black equivalents to previously white dolls, such as astronauts. Barbie and G.I. Joe appeared as Afro-Americans, while Remco put on the market such supposedly realistic black dolls as Baby-Grow-a-Tooth and Li'l Winking Winny, the latter with an Afro hairstyle.

Other popular toys during the decade included James Bond dolls and cars. During the early 1960s, JFK coloring books helped millions of young children learn more about the young president and his family. A child's version of disposable pop art was available with the Etch-A-Sketch, which permitted drawing on a screen by turning two knobs; shaking the screen removed the picture in preparation for the next creation. "Mr. Machine" was a robot that children could take apart and, at least in theory, reassemble without tools. The toys, of course, went on and on, in an unlimited stream.

Active Hobbies

A variety of noteworthy hobbies in the 1960s, some of them closely allied to sports and games, occupied large numbers of Americans. The most physical of these pastimes included bowling, sailing, surfing, skateboarding, and touch football. If tennis at the beginning of the decade was a country-club sport, bowling, in the minds of many, was strictly a lowbrow and low-income pastime. In reality, large numbers of people who deviated from one or both of those categories enjoyed bowling. Its popularity was sufficient to induce ABC to begin televising tournaments in the early 1960s. Don Carter, Billy Hardwick, and Dick Weber were the most prominent male bowlers in the 1960s, with Carter twice named Male Bowler of the Year during the decade, and Hardwick and Weber winning or sharing that distinction three times each. Among women, Shirley Garms was Bowler of the Year in 1961 and 1962, with Dotty Fothergill achieving that distinction in the final two years of the decade. Less accomplished but no less enthusiastic were the many men and women who bowled, informally with friends or relatives, or in leagues, at a local bowling alley. Teams often were sponsored by a business, which received advertising on the backs of the team members' shirts.

Americans who favored outdoor hobbies could take their lead from the Kennedy administration, which increased the popularity of both sailing and touch football during the early 1960s. It was not unusual to see photographs of President Kennedy skippering his family sloop off Hyannis Port, family members aboard, with daughter Caroline sometimes sitting in his lap helping to keep the boat on course. The coastlines, rivers, and lakes of the United States meanwhile offered relaxation and adventure to millions of less famous boaters. Touch football was another Kennedy pastime, with Attorney General and later Senator Robert Kennedy often in the middle of the game. Hardly a sport for sissies, touch football, Kennedy style, was a rugged and highly competitive endeavor shared by enthusiasts on college campuses and residential lawns.

Surfing and Skateboarding

Few outdoors activities are more associated with the 1960s than surfing. An ancient sport that almost died out in the nineteenth century, surfing was reborn in Hawaii early in the twentieth century and became popular in California during the middle of the century. Surfers were an important division of the counterculture of the 1960s, adopting a distinctive attire (typically striped shirts, white jeans, and sunglasses for the males), a peculiar jargon (phrases like "daddy-o" and "kook"), and a fanatical core of true believers in sufficient numbers to warrant their own magazines (e.g., *Surfer*, started in 1960 and still in existence at the beginning of the new century). So popular was surfing, even among millions of people, not all of them young, who never came within yelling distance of a wave, that it inspired a new genre of surfing movies and gave rise to a unique kind of music (called "surf music") transported around the world by the Beach Boys and other groups. Among the songs glorifying surfing were the Beach Boys' "Surfin' USA" and Jan and Dean's "Surf City."

Skateboards evolved from roller skates but actually have more to do with surfing than roller-skating. In the early 1960s, surfers devised an earthbound version of the surfboard to keep in practice when they were away from the waves. By 1963, skateboards had caught on and have stayed around ever since. The original mass-marketed skateboards were made of wood or plastic with wheels underneath; the board is controlled by knees and shifts in body weight to simulate the act of surfing.

Still other outdoor activities were much practiced in the 1960s. A 1966 poll showed approximately fifty-nine million bikers, forty million volleyball players (many of whom played indoors in gyms), and thirty-six million fishers and campers in the United States. Many people also took up jogging, an activity not often seen prior to the 1960s. More than a few of the participants were encouraged in these activities by the call of young President John F. Kennedy in 1961 for Americans to exercise more and become more physically fit.

Quiet Hobbies

Americans who preferred their hobbies indoors had many options, one of which was collecting baseball cards, which remained popular with young baseball fans. Buying packages of cards with pink gum continued in the 1960s, as youngsters looked for their heroes: Willie Mays, Hank Aaron, Mickey Mantle, Sandy Koufax, Bob Gibson, Tom Seaver, Frank Robinson, and many others. Although collecting baseball cards remained primarily a love-of-the-game hobby throughout the decade, the commercialization of card collecting had already started. The pivotal moment in this transformation was the publication of Jefferson Burdick's *The American Card Catalog* in 1967. From then on, card condition, price, and value began to shove aside the old traditions of collecting, trading, and playing imaginative games with the cards. Even young fans started to look at baseball cards as financial investments.

Building model planes and ships remained popular hobbies, primarily with boys, but also with some adults. With the space race blossoming in the 1960s, space vehicles joined lower-flying aircraft on tabletops with diagrams and bottles of glue. Scientifically inclined youngsters also enjoyed science kits, which were especially popular as Christmas presents from parents anxious to encourage their children's academic pursuits.

Photography received a boost as a hobby from development by Kodak of its Instamatic camera in 1963, which used a cartridge and required no real expertise. The musically inclined increasingly turned toward the guitar, mirroring the resurgence of folk music among professionals.

Some of the hobbies already mentioned were at least borderline sports. Watching professional, college, and Olympic sports was a hobby shared by many millions in person or through the media of radio and television.

The Liberation of Women's Fashion

Blanche Linden-Ward and Carol Hurd Green

Blanche Linden-Ward is the author of *Silent City on a Hill*, a historical look at Boston's Mt. Auburn Cemetery. Carol Hurd Green is the coauthor of a book on American women writers. The following excerpt is taken from their book about the rise of feminine self-awareness in the 1960s. In this collective work, Linden-Ward and Green show how women of that decade utilized fashion to gain a stronger sense of self and, thus, gain more control over their social identity.

Beginning with the sophisticated styles popularized by First Lady Jacqueline Kennedy and continuing through to the daring of the miniskirt, the authors show a clear trend in fashion that reflected a general liberation in ideas about proper attire. In previous decades, women's fashions could be elegant yet prudish, but in the 1960s, fashion no longer remained merely a means to enhance a woman's outwardly appearance. The decade reveled in political and sexual awareness, and woman's appearance—especially among young women—became a way of expressing a more liberated identity. While the miniskirt was revealing and therefore bespoke open sexuality, counterculture fashions of the late 1960s denoted political rebellion.

RAPIDLY CHANGING DRESS STYLES THROUGH the sixties provide a measure of the transformation of attitudes of and about women; but changes often were more "cosmetic"

■

Blanche Linden-Ward and Carol Hurd Green, *American Women in the 1960s: Changing the Future*. New York: Twayne, 1993. Copyright © 1993 by Twayne Publishers. All rights reserved. Reproduced by permission of The Gale Group.

than real indices of social and economic status. Media focus on women's presentation of self trivialized or glamorized but rarely reflected or instigated real life changes. Still, when women were questioned about the greatest changes they experienced in the sixties, one response almost unanimously identified dress.

As first lady, Jacqueline Kennedy established an ideal of youthful fashion sophistication, inaugurating a new era by wearing Oleg Cassini's designer clothes—over 300 outfits from 1960 to 1963. Her image of modern female beauty contrasted dramatically with the dowdiness of her predecessor, Mamie Eisenhower. The carefully scripted "Jackie Look" was young, poised, cosmopolitan, elegant, yet simple—calculated to convey the impression of "Camelot," although Cassini interpreted the linear, architectural, A-line silhouette of an "Egyptian princess" for this woman with a Nefertiti head and "sphinxlike quality." Cassini intended the "Jackie Look" to be "simple, charmingly young and innocent. It was unpretentious, well-cut, and implied, 'I am not going to use fashion as a weapon to impress.'"

Conservative Looks

The Jackie Look, echoed and reinforced by [actress] Audrey Hepburn, influenced the way stylish American women dressed. Box-jacketed suits and dresses with sheath and A-line skirts replaced the crinolined, hourglass figures of the fifties and endured through the decade. A single large button or two closed a jacket or coat. Kneecaps discreetly showed below hems, more leg than since World War II. Fashion critic Jean Krueger Neal noted that knee-length skirts were marketed as "part of contemporary life, a 'necessity' in the fast-moving world of modern women."

Through the first half of the decade, genteel and middle-class ladies' fashions worn by young and old included hats, "crisply" starched white collars, and gloves. Young women going to New York jobs as late as 1966 knew it was necessary and proper to wear gloves in public, even on the subway. Jackie Kennedy's signature pillbox hat, created by Cassini for her bouffant hairdo, was widely imitated. The First Lady made news in 1962 when she wore a wide, flat hairbow instead of a hat at a Washington luncheon, signalling rejection of the hat as necessity for the well-dressed lady. By 1964, fashion leaders like Betty Furness made headbands a way to be "classy look-ing" and "dressy" without wearing a hat. . . .

While the "Jackie Look" had an enormous influence, the Ivy-League or "collegiate look" persisted into the sixties. It in-

As first lady, Jacqueline Kennedy brought a youthful, sophisticated style to the White House. Her designer dresses set trends that swept the nation.

cluded matching pastel tweed or flannel, A-line or "slim" skirts and delicate wool cardigan or pullover sweaters—"Villager" or "Bobbie Brooks" clothes, the former more prestigious. More informal dress or "sports wear," associated with the collegiate look, featured straight, plaid "guaranteed to bleed" [to fade and blend when washed] Indian madras cotton skirts, bermuda shorts, or plaid woolen kilts—an updated anglophilia. As Ellen Melinkoff observes, "There was a minor but continuing conservative strain all through the sixties, although it never made the front pages."

Over the course of the sixties many young women rejected the poise, posture, and proper ladylike behavior and dress inculcated through the middle class; but evidence of nonconformity in dress appeared among some teens as early as in the fifties. Secondary school administrations frowned at the rise of teen culture, especially among girls, and reacted to fads and fashions with codified dress regulations, which had formerly been a matter of unwritten custom. Girls were forbidden to appear in high school wearing slacks, let alone "dungarees." Many schools banned make-up or placed limits on excessively styled hair—both to regulate appearance and to limit the time girls spent grooming themselves in the "ladies' room." Even before the rise of the new feminism, young women organized to expand their rights to vary dress options. At Battle Creek Central High School in Michigan in 1963, a petition drive successfully won for girls a monthly "Slacks Day," when dressy pants were permitted, but not the tighter, shorter-legged capris or Jax pants that replaced fifties "pedal pushers." In most sororities at the University of Michigan until 1968, girls could only wear pants to lunch if they were art students with studio courses.

Through the decade, even after the appearance of the first bellbottoms in 1961, most women's pants fit snugly at the top, fastened by a flat zipper in the back or side, but not with fly fronts, considered too "mannish"; sleek-look stretch pants with stirrup foot were popular. In 1962 British designer Mary Quant presented the first designs for a "trouser suit." The tailored but feminine and mod pantsuit inspired by Yves Saint Laurent that could be worn on dressy occasions did not catch on until the fall of 1967. Often trouser suits included tunics, like mini-dresses over bellbottom pants. Pants were worn primarily by the young, however; and it was not until the decade's end and later that mature women made them part of their wardrobe. . . .

Quant's Revolution

Beginning in 1955, British designer Quant, a former art student and proponent of the ultra-modern or "mod," created a youth market in fashion. With her boyfriend Alexander Plunket Greene, she produced her own short, skinny pinafores and tunics, simple jackets, scanty underwear, and outrageous accessories—a new "swinger" style that quickly swept America. Quant saw her customers as liberated sexually and socially, representatives "of a whole new spirit." In 1960 a few cosmopolitan Americans discovered Quant's knee-length jumpers, intended to have "the look of the precocious child." *Seventeen* featured her spring fashions in 1961; and in 1962, her straight, short, box-like dresses of huge, checkered fabric squares sparked American interest in the "shift" dress, actively marketed by J.C. Penney in an attempt to give its stores a new youthful, fashionable image. The loose, light, waistless "shift" or "sack" dress was popular in the summer of 1963. Melinkoff remembers feeling "the first tremors of the youthquake." Quant introduced American women "to the fashion-is-fun, life-as-theater" way of living.

Quant revolutionized women's fashions in 1965 with her miniskirt, four to seven inches above the knee, not to be worn by the inhibited because of the way it limited movement for those who did not choose to "show all." Her message was: "You'll see the world differently from inside a mod minidress than in a shirtwaist and girdle." One critic observed, "we looked like . . . dolls. . . . Twenty-year-olds no longer looked thirty; they now looked ten." Another explained, "Quant invented the girl." She hoped to make dress transcend conventional propriety and status: "Sex is taken for granted. They talk candidly about everything from puberty to homosexuality. The girls are curiously feminine but their femininity lies in their attitude rather than in their appearance" whether dukes', doctors', or dockers' daughters. "They are not interested in status symbols. They don't worry about accents or class. . . . Snobbery has gone out of fashion, and in our shops you will find duchesses jostling with typists to buy the same dresses. . . .

They represent the whole new spirit . . . a classless spirit that has grown out of the Second World War.". . . .

Quant's black tights and boots with the mini-skirt eventually gave way in America to the vogue for fishnet stockings and Go-Go boots, often in white—the signature color of Paris designer André Corrèges, who accesorized his finely cut, futuristic, vinyl microminis with head-hugging helmet hats and boots, suggestive of the space age. Go-Go Girls, wearing short shorts called "hot pants," danced in cages on television shows like *Laugh-In* and *Hootenanny* and in bar clubs in major cities. The term "à go-go" originated in the first years of the sixties, meaning "As much as you like; to your heart's content; galore," according to the *Random House Dictionary of the English Language*—a feminine version of the culture of abundance, the optimistic belief in the modern to replace the traditional.

Quant also dictated a new look in make-up—a cosmetological revolution. Pale pink, pearlescent lipstick, nearly white, or nude lip gloss replaced mothers' bright red. Sheer, colorless powder and a light, powder blush replaced the thick liquid or pancake foundation and rouge of the older generation. Eye make-up became heavier than ever before with black eyeliner on bottom and top lids for a wide-eyed appearance. Long false eyelashes became standard for many young women. . . .

Revealing Apparel

Another London designer, Barbara ("Biba") Hulanicki, had launched her own influential neo-romantic or "hippie" line in 1964, popularizing "French cut" tee-shirts with narrow little shoulders or cut-away armholes, maintaining that "if you looked narrow across the top then you looked narrow all over, and these designs suited the new Twiggy shape of girl to perfection." The new feminine ideal became a "waiflike body with thin shoulders and hollow chest, a pale face with huge, elaborately made-up eyes"—later to be termed anorexic. A version of this look appeared in the controversial film *Bonnie and Clyde* (1967) as Faye Dunaway revived thirties styles—the wearing of berets, slinky dresses cut on a bias, and tiny, rib-hugging, short-sleeved sweaters. These tight "Poor Boys," introduced in America in 1965, were part of the new "prêt-à-porter" trend, ready-to-wear clothing copied from designer styles in London and Paris. . . .

Even before Quant, an avant garde sensibility—the desire to shock the bourgeoisie—had taken hold in fashion, sparked by the Vienna-born, California designer Rudi Gernreich. . . .

Gernreich's "no-bra bra," a flimsy, transparent garment providing minimal support, spurred competitors to devise backless bras, sideless bras, and even frontless bras. Warner's lingerie marketed a skin-tight, flesh-colored, nylon body stocking in summer of 1964. In April 1965 *Playboy* proclaimed "an age of limitless revelation. . . . Today's woman, to the delight of males who suffered through the femme-concealing fashions of the fifties, has rediscovered that sex and style can be synonymous." In January 1968, before radical feminists in America dumped (but did not burn!) their bras in protest at the Miss America Pageant, Yves Saint Laurent showed a model in braless transparent blouse in his spring collection. Young American feminists might be said to have co-opted bralessness, albeit with ordinary tee-shirts as covering, from high fashion. . . .

By 1969, given the trend towards exposure, Quant predicted that "body cosmetics and certainly pubic hair—which we can now view in the cinema and on the stage—will become a fashion emphasis, although not necessarily blatant." Newspapers named the summer of 1970 "the nudest ever." [Fashion writer Brigid] Keenan called it "the grand finale of a long, slow striptease" going on all through the sixties. "It started at the very beginning of the decade when we stepped out of our corsets and roll-ons, and the rigmarole of stockings and suspenders was replaced by flesh-colored tights." Seventies fashions did not go any further.

Signs of Rebellion

After 1965, the young who questioned authority rejected mainstream ideals of appearance. Susan Gill, a New York designer since 1966, describes the second half of the decade as unprecedented—fashion changed "so fast, as never before and never since." The last years of the decade saw a diversity of styles come and go, new and then obsolete in a single season, every six months—wide-legged, mannish "buffalo" pants worn with "Poor Boys"; gaucho suits with mid-calf, skirt-like legs; long "maxi" coats worn over mini skirts; common men's jeans tucked into boots; real, tall, leather boots for women for winter instead of the old, dainty, high-heeled, dressy boots ringed with fur around the ankle. Young women began shopping at Army-Navy surplus stores. Faded and tattered denim, bell-bottom jeans—called "dungarees" by the older generation—became universal among those rejecting middle-class fashions. Gill considered each "another sort of rebellion . . . once we women got the freedom." In the winter of 1967, fashion arbiters called for ankle-length coats over mini-skirts; and in 1968, they pushed mid-ankle-length "midi" skirts. But many women rebelled. A writer for *Harper's Bazaar*, observed, "Fashion was stripped of its dictatorial powers in 1968 by a revolutionary assertion of individuality. Stylish women throughout the world put the catch phrase 'do your own thing' into practice by replacing the safe couture-approved dress with costumey, role-playing clothes that were outward projections of their inner selves."

Repeated innovations diversified clothing; and with the appearance of the midcalf-length "midi" and ankle-length "maxi" skirts in 1968, women had new freedom to customize their own personal look. Long skirts appeared on counterculture women before designers attempted to popularize the midi and the maxi skirt, and they persisted well into the seventies. Those on limited budgets discovered they could quickly and cheaply create an outfit by hemming and putting elastic for the waist in a double panel of fabric. The young also liked the bare midriff look, accentuated in the last years of the decade by hip-hugger pants, low slung at navel rather than waist level. As Ellen Melinkoff remembers, "To show off the midriff was a statement of freedom." Even hippy inspired clothes—loosely crocheted tops, vests, and dresses—revealed considerable skin.

The popular peasant look favored kaftans, ponchos, gauzy blouses, and rustic beads imported from third world countries like India, Peru, Bali, and Morocco. By the end of the decade, wearing such clothes suggested sympathy with those peoples. . . . New ethnic boutiques and "head shops" in college towns and cities sold imports. In the second half of the decade, young women began piercing their ears; often performing the task themselves in dorm rooms using ice cubes, corks, common needles, and alcohol—a do-it-yourself, countercultural ritual for many. . . .

More than ever before, women in the sixties displayed their

ideology, philosophy, politics, or anti-hierarchical style through choice of clothing and presentation of self. According to [author] Joan Cassell, one could immediately distinguish a women's-rights feminist, a member of a group like NOW, from an advocate of women's liberation by the "uniform" worn. . . .

Funky Fashions

No one epitomized that radical eclecticism of late-sixties women dress better than Janis Joplin, whose custom-made hippie garb came from seamstresses and designers like Lydall Erb of New York. The folk-rock and hippie vogues in music were matched by a taste for "funky" or old-fashioned clothes or styles recycled as new counter-cultural dress. Hippie women reverted to the crafts of their grandmothers or more distant female ancestors—elaborately embroidering old, worn denim pants or patchwork skirts with intricate, idiosyncratic designs; crocheting vests and shawls; quilting used fabric scraps in gaudy patterns inspired by a psychedelic sensibility; tie-dying T-shirts in clashing, "electric" colors. What they could not make, they bought. The counter-culture created a new sort of folk art of dress that was anti-modern, favoring the styles and crafts of a mythological, idealized, preindustrial frontier past, where women broke away from genteel rules to live a more simple, authentic, and cruder existence while still retaining their old domestic skills with needle and thread.

Joplin shunned make-up and seldom washed her long brown hair. Her clothes, often vests and pants of embroidered velvet and denim, were hand-made. She wore granny glasses, gaudy beads, bracelets, rings, and feathers from second-hand stores. Joplin told one reporter, "Like man, I really don't give a damn about clothes. Basically, clothes are a facade, nothing more. I groove on my clothes now because I have to." Fashion was for comfort and freedom, she exclaimed, "Anything that interferes with my thing, baby, forget it." She insisted, "The secret is freedom, and that means no bras or girdles. You got to do what you want to do and wear what you want to wear. Everybody is so hung up on the matching game—the shoes have to match the bag which matches the coat and dress. But the big question is, is it matching your soul?" . . .

Despite the sixties' fashion vagaries and a growing feminist consciousness, the popularity of beauty pageants still promulgated a mainstream, traditional ideal of female beauty. Beauty contests, large and small, took place over five thousand times a year on the international, national, state, and local level. . . . The 1962 National College Queen Pageant idealized "the well-rounded average," chosen after competition in blouse-ironing, hamburger cooking, serving judges coffee, decorating sandals, and debating the "right and wrong hairstyles." Little Miss America was chosen from girls aged four to eight based on "beauty of face, figure, charm, poise, and personality." Most contests asked for talent but emphasized a slim, well-groomed look in swimsuit and evening dress. All emulated Miss America, chosen annually since 1921. The "beauty queen" inevitably promoted many products during her year's "reign," with most proceeds going to the competition organizers. Girls trained intensively for beauty pageants, like budding athletes, from an early age.

Young girls also received training in older ideals of fashionable, feminine dress and presentation of self from the Barbie doll, first marketed by Mattel in 1959 and named after the daughter of company founders Ruth and Eliot Handler. With blond hair, pointed breasts, and long legs, Barbie presented a stereotyped, exaggerated ideal of the perpetually teenaged prom queen or fashion model. In 1961, a boyfriend/companion doll, Ken, was introduced and then girlfriends Stacey, Casey, and Midge as well as little sister Skipper. Girls could collect outfits and accessories for miniature role playing. . . . New editions of Barbie kept up with the latest hairstyles—changing from the ponytail of 1959, to the bubble of 1961, to the flip in 1964, and finally long, straight hair in 1967. Mattel even gave Barbie a black friend, Christie, more in an attempt to tap a larger market of blacks than as a nod to integration.

Black Is Beautiful: Redefining Beauty in Black America

Arthur Marwick

Arthur Marwick is an emeritus professor of history at
the Open University in England, where he codirected
the Sixties Research Group until it was disbanded in
2003. In the following excerpt, Marwick discusses how
ideals of beauty changed in the African American community during the 1960s. According to Marwick, the
predominant images of beauty had been traditionally
drawn from white America, and in the 1960s most
television and periodical advertisers followed that convention. But in the 1950s and 1960s, the era which
brought greater attention to the black community, new
African American periodicals emerged to both influence and gauge the trends of black consumers. Marwick examines *Ebony*, one of the flagship publications,
to explore how and why blacks turned from modeling
their own self-images on white standards to embracing
the notion of natural, African American beauty. In
Marwick's estimation, the most obvious example of this
transformation took place among black women who
went from imitation of white ideals to a proud declara-
tion that "black is beautiful."

IN MAKING BEAUTY A MATTER OF PUBLIC INTER-
est and concern, an important part was played by the explosion
in mass communications, particularly television and the new

■

Arthur Marwick, *The Sixties: Cultural Revolution in Britain, France, Italy, and the United
States, c. 1958–c. 1974.* Oxford, UK: Oxford University Press, 1998. Copyright © 1998
by Arthur Marwick. All rights reserved. Reproduced by permission of the publisher.

style of advertising associated with Madison Avenue in New York, but also developing semi-independently in Paris and in London. Advertising may well be thought the very soul of deceit, the sworn enemy of frankness and openness. But the new advertising of the sixties was also bold, uninhibited, witty, naturalistic, and rather in the manner of some of the sixties novels, explicit, and, of course, fully exploitative of the appeal of a beautiful face and figure, whether female or male. The beauty was that of anonymous models rather than of people of established status (though modelling quickly became a means of achieving status). The new advertising was involving, rather than distant and authoritarian; it advertised the artefacts of the consumer society rather than the quack medicines of the past. International beauties continued to be recruited into everyone's consciousness through film, but television, situated in the family sitting room, is far more intimate and engaging than film: in that process of comparison, contrast, and choice on which all sexual selection, in some degree, is based, the beautiful person on the small screen in the sitting room is an even more disturbing phenomenon than the beautiful person at some distance on the large screen.

The new fashions displayed the natural endowments of youth, just as the new internationalism displayed the varieties of beauty from many different countries. How did all this affect the Afro-Americans . . . ? My main source is *Ebony*, by the end of the 1950s a large and lavishly produced monthly colour magazine, owned by a black family and produced by a mixed staff on which blacks were in a majority, selling three-quarters of a million copies, and probably reaching a total of 5,000,000 readers. The quality of the writing and of the photojournalism in *Ebony* is very high indeed; the tone is liberal, commonsense, strongly in favour of black civil rights, and deeply proud of black achievements within the framework of American society. (To see *Ebony*, or any other journal for that matter, as the voice of all blacks would, of course, be absurd.) Consistently, there is throughout a very heavy emphasis on questions of personal appearance discussed at two quite different levels. Most of the items are relatively trivial in nature, though informed with a sharp practicality and wit, apparently being mainly aimed at black women exercised by the problems of securing a husband;

but some articles firmly tie in the question of personal appearance with that of civil rights—as blacks become more assertive and more powerful, it is argued, they must present an appearance of which all blacks can be proud.

Following White Standards of Beauty

Ebony carried a large number of advertisements featuring black models; it also carried a very large number of advertisements for hair-straighteners, skin-whiteners, and many other beauty aids designed to help blacks look as much like whites as possible. The orthodoxy had been that black women, if not black men, should always straighten their hair. As well as regular articles on grooming and make-up and on fashion, there were frequent articles on beauty competitions, on the personal appearance of famous black women, on 'best-dressed Negro women', on such questions as 'What is the best age for beauty?' (treated with typical wit—'beauty experts say women, like wines, improve with age', but 'science, skin specialists, even Doctor Kinsey, have not succeeded in dousing the average male's enthusiasm for a young bustling companion'), and each year, in June, an article on 'eligible bachelors'. These last features do not in any way, as one might at first imagine, take the line that men should be assessed on their looks—in fact most of those selected were earnest, bespectacled, and distinctly unglamorous, what they stood for being primarily economic success; the cutting edge of every article was what these men were looking for in a woman. Yet even in this exercise *Ebony* managed some of its usual double-edged wit: 'Baseball player Willy McCovey, 24,' one of the 1962 eligible bachelors, 'of the San Francisco Giants, describes his ideal woman as sports minded, honest and understanding, with charm and beauty. Being a realist he says he'll sacrifice a little beauty if the woman has all the other qualities.' The summing up for 1964 was: 'As with last year's round-up, the bachelors placed a premium on brains and personality but admitted that beauty still rates a strong consideration'. The summary for the following year gives the same emphasis to intellectual and other sterling qualities, but then adds with significant use of block capitals, 'NOT ONE OBJECTS TO BEAUTY'.

At the core of all this lies the assumption (never in any way stated explicitly) that a black woman will have a struggle to attain even a plain, though economically successful and upwardly mobile, black man, and that indeed (this is very deeply buried in the text) she will be lucky to do so. Her energy should be directed to making herself as much like a white woman as possible. It is recognized that a black man may occasionally marry a white woman; this will happen when the black man is economically very successful so that the marriage will actually represent an economic and social advancement for the white woman concerned. The question is not broached of whether it is a sign of status for a black man to manage to marry a white woman; nor is there any hint of the even more distressing possibility that black men might actually find most white women more beautiful than most black women. However, in December 1965 there was a sad letter from a black girl ('I'm considered pretty') lamenting that black men were going after white women and ignoring black ones, while white men were definitely not going after black girls. When, at the end of the decade, Hollywood did get round to treating this issue, in *Guess Who's Coming to Dinner* . . . , the relationship was black man–white woman, the man mature and very successful, the woman very young.

Prizing Talent over Beauty

The successful black women featured by *Ebony* all had the 'whitified' look; this is particularly evident on the cover and illustrated article of October 1961 on—and the pun may have been intended—'*Ebony* Fashion Fair Beauties'. Wherever black girls did well in beauty competitions open to both blacks and whites *Ebony* was there reporting enthusiastically; invariably what the black girls won was never more than a consolation prize, but then, as seen in *Ebony*'s highly professional photography, they were never particularly beautiful (in the 'modern' sense of external physical beauty). The puzzle is explained when it is appreciated that these competitions featured 'talent'—usually singing ability—as well as mere physical beauty. In the summer of 1965 a 'Negro girl' did win a victory of sorts, but again the story, under the reading of 'Negro Girl in "Miss America" Race: Voice Student Wins "Miss Rochester" title', was more revealing than the editors seemed to realize:

Sarah says she didn't know her measurements were 36, 24, 35 until judges told her, adds: 'I guess they are right.' Classmate Carol Gane was Sarah's runner-up for title. Second balloting gave title to Sarah after a tie between the two. Girls were judged on five qualities: bathing suit appearance, talent (50%), formal gown appearance, charm and poise. Said one judge: 'It was close between Carol and Sarah. But Sarah placed very high on talent.'

My deduction from all this would be that black women were not really expected to look beautiful, though they were expected to be able to sing. Some black women, of course, *were* very beautiful, and in the less prejudiced international scene at the Cannes Film Festival black models won titles as International Queen of the Cannes Film Festival in 1959, and again in 1960.

It is 1966 which emerges as the fulcrum year, and I can set this up nicely by referring to an article entitled 'Instant Hair' in the November 1965 issue of *Ebony*. This, significantly enough, was a witty and light-hearted article on a topic which had always been of deathly seriousness for black women. Referring to her own 'crowning glory', the author notes that, in imitation of 'the Beatle Baez look' (in her own way the American singer of protest songs Joan Baez had an impact comparable to that of the Beatles), whites were now straightening out their curly hair: 'the finest human hair is European . . . American hair, they say, is too brittle for wig-making. And Negro hair? We are basically consumers, remember? Not producers'. The article is essentially a celebration of the many varieties of wig now available. What is most significant is that this article provoked a pointed, and even angry, reader's letter, published in the January 1966 issue:

It seems to me there is an on-going need for practical fashion and beauty information for women of color. I am sick of seeing negro women 'lift' make-ups intended for the 'natural' look on white skin, transformed to the 'unnatural' look on us. . . . I have seen enough bleached blondes to make me everlastingly determined not to lead this one life in such a horrifying, stupefying and shocking manner. Nor will white lipstick ever enhance the natural beauty of my lips. . . . With a daughter approaching her teens, I've become very conscious of this especially when she asks, is it true, blondes have more fun? Maybe—but who the devil wants to be the object of it, especially behind one's back?

Prettier or Just Whiter?

In the very next issue (no doubt planned several months in advance) *Ebony* nevertheless plunged straight on with a full-colour cover entitled 'Are Negro Girls Getting Prettier?'. The six models on the cover and most of the women photographed inside were of the usual *Ebony* type. The verbal message inside was along the lines: 'Experts say better nutrition, grooming, know-how have brought improvement.' Gone, claimed the article 'are the spindly legs, sagging bosoms, unruly rumps and ungroomed heads that marred many a potential lovely of yester year. Such common flaws have been displaced by a feminine refinement, both facial and physical, that has elevated today's young lady of hue to a place of prominence among the most pulchritudinous'. The article provoked some stinging letters: The first quoted below is essentially traditional in attitude, but the other three are bombshells:

> How dare you? We Negro women are the only women in the world who don't get any praise for our beauty. Now you decide to write an article called, 'Are Negro Girls Getting Prettier?' We have been pretty all along. Just up until a few years ago we had no access to cosmetics, wigs, etc. White women have been using these things for years, and could afford them I might add. I suggest you rephrase your article to: 'Are Negro People (male or female) Getting Smarter?' According to that article you published, no—dumber.

> Your February, 1966 issue of the magazine asks the question: 'Are Negro Girls Getting Prettier?' Why don't you put some Negro girls so we can see (instead of half white)? Are you ashamed of the Negro girl? Or do you go along with the white man's premise that a Negro can only be good-looking when he/she is mixed with the white race?

> The cover of your (Feb.) issue delivered today made me (and a lot of other people I'll wager) wince. It should be titled 'Are Negro Girls Getting Whiter?' Come to my high school and I'll show you some girls to photograph who will illustrate, I believe, that Negro girls have always been pretty.

Yes, Negro girls are getting prettier! But your cover is a refutation of the statement. The majority of us are dark brown with bold features. The girls on your cover do illustrate various types of beauty. You have, however, omitted several other beautiful types which are much more typical of our people.

The Natural Look

In June 1966 *Ebony* made the break. The cover heading was: 'The Natural Look: New Mode for Negro Women.' The cover photograph was of a stunningly beautiful black woman, an exquisitely proportioned and intensely appealing face, surmounted by close-cropped fuzzy hair. For once this was no model or blues singer; it was Diana Smith, a 20-year-old Chicago civil rights worker. The main article inside is headed: 'The Natural Look: Many Negro Women Reject White Standards of Beauty'.

> A Frenchman who had been in this country but a short time was astonished to encounter on the street one day a shapely, brown-skinned woman whose close-cropped, rough textured hair was in marked contrast to that of Brigitte Bardot—or any other woman he's ever seen. Intrigued by her extraordinarily curly locks, he rushed up to her and blurted in Gallic impulsiveness: 'But I thought only Negro *men* had kinky hair!'

> His prior observation had not been entirely incorrect, for, throughout the ages, American women of color have conspired to conceal the fact that their hair is not quite like any other. This key element in the black female's mystique was, until recently, challenged only by a few bold bohemians, a handful of entertainers and dancing ethnologists like Pearl Primus, whose identification with the exotic placed them beyond the pale of convention. But for the girl in the street—the coed, the career woman, the housewife, the matron and even the maid who had been born with 'bad' or kinky hair, the straightening comb and chemical processes seemingly offered the only true paths to social salvation.

> Not so today, for an increasing number of Negro women are turning their backs on traditional concepts of style and beauty by wearing their hair in its naturally kinky state.

Though they remain a relatively small group, confined primarily to the trend-making cities of New York and Chicago, they are frequently outspoken, and always aware of definite reasons why they decided to 'go natural'.

'We, as black women, must realise that there is beauty in what we are, without having to make ourselves into something we aren't', contends Suzi Hill, 23-year-old staff field worker with the Southern Christian Leadership Conference.

'Economics is a part ot it too,' notes Diana Smith, 20, another stalwart at [Martin Luther] King's urban headquarters where natural hair has become a badge of honor. 'It's a shame, but many poor Negro housewives take money that should be grocery money and use it to get their hair done. Now that wigs have come along, I see kids whose families are on Welfare, wearing them to high school—wigs and raggedy coats'.

Of the letters printed in reaction to this article (in the August issue), eight expressed strong hostility to the idea of the natural look, seven strong support, though one of these noted that opinion among those with whom the writer had discussed the matter was overwhelmingly against; two further letters did not express an opinion either way. The arguments against tended to ask why, since white women spent hours beautifying themselves, and usually started out with hair whose 'natural state is stringy and straggly', black women should not do the same, or suggested that the next stage would be grass huts and 'rings through our noses'. The most positive response with respect to the natural look actually being appealing, as distinct from racially correct, came from a white, male reader:

To me the women photographed to illustrate it were among the most beautiful I had ever seen. The 'white standards of beauty' they reject are the same standards that choke our cities and suburbs with garish ugliness. May we all become more natural . . . in every way!

The most pungent female expression of hostility was:

It may not be a secret that our hair is of the so-called 'bad' type and gives us trouble some times, but let's assure this: 'We don't have to go around PROVING it!'

Black Is Beautiful

Over a year later *Ebony* returned to the topic, with the cover featuring 'Natural Hair—New Symbol of Race Pride', but this time showing leading male singers and actors. For the first time reference is made to the new slogan of the black liberation movement, 'Black is Beautiful'. An appreciation was developing that to attain some kind of acceptability it was not necessary for black women to pass themselves off as imitation white women, and that some black women were extremely beautiful in their own right and in their own style. Inevitably, many blacks, men and women, like many whites, remained plain or ugly. And just as the miniskirt and hot pants of the sixties gave way to other fashions, so many black women continued to opt for Caucasian hair styles. (It should be noted that many blacks have a considerable admixture of white genes, with the result that their hair is often naturally straight anyway.) The enduring point is that new choices had opened up, and beauty was being recognized as a natural physical quality, not something related to the slavish imitation of convention.

The actual personal appearance of men, as well as their clothing styles, was receiving more and more attention. In March 1964 a top film actor had this written about him:

> While most people who have seen him agree that his boyish face belies his 37 years, they would disagree with his self-appraisal of 'averageness'. At six-foot-two, he is four inches taller than the average American male and there is nothing average about the feline grace of contained power with which he moves his mean frame across the stage or screen. Undoubtedly one of Poitier's biggest assets in today's climate of changing racial values is the dark complexion of his handsome, clean-cut face.

Sidney Poitier had himself modestly said: 'I am blessed with a kind of physical averageness that fits Negroes between 18 and 40. I look like what producers are looking for'. The real point was that Poitier's colour was no longer an obstacle to the perception on all sides that he was a very handsome man. And whatever the confusion still attending black women in America, one, a young woman from Detroit, had established herself on the European scene by mid-1966 as one of the most photographed models of the time: Donyale Luna.

This really does drive home the point that the many varieties of beauty were now being recognized. Such being the way of the fashion industry, and such the way of the mass media, it is true that one type might be very strongly featured at one point in time and another at another; but many different types of beauty were in and out of the headlines throughout the sixties. There was less pressure than ever before to conform to dictates and conventions in this matter.

CHAPTER

2

EXAMINING POP CULTURE

Film and Television

Films Document a Turbulent Decade

David Sanjek

In the following excerpt, David Sanjek examines the films of the 1960s. He contends that the allure of these films lies in the fact that they simultaneously embraced the counterculture and endorsed the status quo. According to Sanjek, the documentary realism that defined such films as *Medium Cool, Easy Rider*, and *Petulia* showed that some of the more provocative directors were trying to analyze the new generation and its motives. For Sanjek, the worst of these became propagandists for the counterculture, the best forced audiences to contemplate their own place within the divisive society. Sanjek is the archives director at Broadcast Music, Inc.

AS THE FILM INDUSTRY FLOUNDERED, AMERICAN society was entering a period of substantial social, political, racial, and cultural transformation. These changes profoundly affected the youth of the United States, demographically the largest element of the filmgoing public. As the decade advanced, Hollywood began, tentatively, to document the ruptures in their world. However, acknowledging and valorizing social change are not the same process. For every *Easy Rider* (1969), there is yet another *Beach Party Bingo* (1965). The commercial cinema was quite ready to exploit countercultural modes of expression, but that did not mean it would censure the ideological presuppositions of the dominant culture. We must not forget that film is a commodity produced by an in-

■

David Sanjek, "Apocalypse Then: Apocalyptic Imagery and Documentary Reality in Films of the 1960s," *Sights on the Sixties*, edited by Barbara L. Tischler. New Brunswick, NJ: Rutgers University Press, 1992. Copyright © 1992 by David Sanjek. Reproduced by permission.

dustrial system; it is dependent upon the investment of speculative capital and therefore seeks to legitimate the status quo. Social tensions and contradictions are minimized if not eradicated. Any questions raised about society's vulnerabilities have to be answered; any criticisms of society have to give way before the inescapable attractions of consumer capitalism. Axel Madsen acknowledged this failure of nerve in American cinema when he wrote:

> What separates Hollywood from European cinema, and constantly widens the Atlantic, is the American myth of the mechanical age that a good film is first of all a film that exhausts all its possibilities. Yet in the arts we live in Nietzschean times, the era of the charm of imperfection, where creators beguile more with what they hint at than with what they achieve. The lack of personal point of view that efficacy implies used to be the strength of American films; today this virtue seems to be a barrier to the future.

Built-In Ambivalence

Despite the applicability of Madsen's comments to most Hollywood films of the period, some produced during the 1960s possess the "charm of imperfection" of which he writes. This is particularly true of those pictures that incorporate a fictional narrative with factual documentation of environments, social movements, or events representative of the period. However, more often than not in the films I discuss here, the fictional and factual material clashes rather than coheres. Their plots, all too often melodramatic, generational conflicts, lack either the substance or the significance of the settings in which they occur. This conflict between content and context leaves the viewer free to choose where to focus attention and gives rise to what Lawrence Alloway has called "media echoes," whereby "the images on the screen are always extending to contemporaneous data off the screen, slurring into a sociological matrix."

What makes many of the films of the period still worthy of our attention is just these "media echoes" that simultaneously affirm and attack the social transformation of the 1960s. Depending upon where the viewer focuses his or her attention, these films are either celebrations of social experimentation or defenses of the status quo. To examine this process I discuss five filmic modes: the grade-B exploitation feature, particularly those documenting the biker and drug subcultures; the "mondo" documentary; the road movie; the campus protest movie; the agit-prop political drama; and the work of expatriate or European directors, including Richard Lester . . . , who bring an outsider's eye to the American scene. Each mode in turn embodies the collision between the desire to contain, if not condemn, and an often inadvertent celebration of the very forces the films undermine. . . .

It is all too easy to underestimate the role of the audience in determining meaning. Consumers can direct their attention to one element of a film, in this case the factual rather than the fictional material, while ignoring another, thereby deliberately recontextualizing the work by appropriating for their own uses what was designed to use them. Films, like all texts, do not possess unitary meanings the audience is designed to uncover. Meanings are produced by concrete viewers receiving images in specific cultural contexts. The spirit and the meaning of the 1960s remain alive in these films because audiences continue to maneuver their way between the tensions the films embody and to appropriate, for their own purposes, the significance of the cultural, political, and social aspirations the films document.

Exploiting the Counterculture

We turn first to the commercial exploitation movie, which Tom Doherty defines as a work that incorporates controversial content, bottom-line bookkeeping, and demographic targeting, and took as an appropriate subject matter the dynamic social changes in American society occurring in the sixties. Two areas of marketable interest to the exploitation filmmaker were the biker culture and the drug scene. The biker culture was first brought to public attention by *The Wild One* (1953) and, for the more informed filmgoer, Kenneth Anger's *Scorpio Rising* (1963), in addition to journalistic reports, including Hunter Thompson's *Hell's Angels: A Strange and Terrible Saga* (1967). The drug scene was known particularly for experimentation with LSD and the corresponding changes in social relations as embodied by the Haight-Ashbury district of San Francisco. The most distinctive cinematic responses to these developments were those of Roger Corman and Richard Rush. Corman, the premier exploitation filmmaker, whose work goes back to 1955 and who had earlier examined the rock and roll scene and helped inaugurate the reinvigorated horror and science fiction genres, focuses on the countercultural revolution in his films *The Wild Angels* (1966) and *The Trip* (1967) which simultaneously salute and censure both the biker culture and the drug scene. This ambivalent perspective is shared by Richard Rush's *Hell's Angels on Wheels* (1967) and *Psych-Out* (1968).

Heavenly Blues (Peter Fonda), the leader of the Wild Angels, is a consummate antihero; while he engages in nihilistic violence, he frowns upon fellow bikers shooting heroin, attempts to constrain their most violent tendencies, and commits himself to the burial of his dead friend, the Loser. Corman's romantic validation of the Angels' antisocial behavior is illustrated stylistically by tracking shots of their riding through the mountains and desert, framing them telephotically against the landscape in a manner reminiscent of classic Western cinematic iconography. However, the predominant tone of the film is one of implicit censure, particularly in the climactic pillaging of a church by the Angels, during which the jagged hand-held photography mirrors the group's lack of control. Even if the film's final line, Blue's nihilistic statement "There's nowhere to go," uttered over the Loser's grave, romantically attempts to see the group as antiheroic, the imagery overwhelmingly validates a nihilistic depiction of the worst of human nature. . . .

Corman's subsequent film, *The Trip*, paints a far more affirmative image of the drug culture as a force for the expansion, not retrogression, of consciousness. Perhaps as a reflection of Corman's own affirmative experience with LSD, Paul Groves (Peter Fonda), a commercial advertisement director, begins to move outside a narcissistic self-involvement as a result of dropping acid, even if the form and substance of his acid visions profoundly resemble commercial advertising imagery and style, suggesting that he has not entirely left behind the world the film rejects. Nonetheless, the film's implicit endorsement of the use of drugs for the expansion of consciousness caused one reviewer to refer to it as a virtual advertisement for LSD. The film's distributor, American International Pictures, perhaps sensing the potential for such a judgement, placed a prefatory admonition against the manufacture and consumption of LSD and optically altered the film's final image by interjecting an image of shattering glass, suggesting that Paul, much as he affirms his experience with his final dialogue, has merely made a Faustian bargain with his body chemistry. Nonetheless, the predominant tone of *The Trip* undermines, if not eradicates, such a judgement.

Richard Rush's *Psych-Out* (1968) presents an equally contradictory depiction of Haight-Ashbury. Its plot line, a melodramatically convoluted tale of a deaf, runaway teenager's search for her brother who is lost among the freaks of San Francisco, is interrupted by sequences documenting elements of that milieu, ranging from the Digger's Free Store, be-ins, and the communal spontaneity of the Fillmore and Avalon Ballroom. It is those sequences that most impress themselves upon the viewer's attention, as the knotty and overly dense plot is an imposition upon the playful environment. The film's final shot illustrates this conflict as a split screen incorporates an image from the film's portentously apocalyptic conclusion with an earlier idyllic image of the playfulness the Haight embodied. This confusion perhaps also reflects the fact that fifteen minutes of footage was edited from the final print. American International Pictures apparently feared being seen as an advocate of alternative social practices.

Peering into Subcultures

The "mondo" movies, so called by reference to the benchmark film *Mondo Cane* (1963), are documentaries that focus on shocking subject matter, the film equivalent of yellow or tabloid journalism. They are clearly meant to shock and/or titillate by allowing the observer privileged access to forbidden environments or ways of life. These films often incorporate all too clearly fabricated footage, but even when they do not, their aim, through portentous and denunciatory narration, is to vitiate any meaning the subject matter might possess. Such is the case with such titles as *Mondo Bizarro* (1966), *Mondo Teeno* (1967), *Mondo Mod* (1967), and *Mondo Hollywood* (1967) which examine American and international youth subcultures. However, it is altogether possible for a spectator, particularly one appreciative of, or committed to, the way of life under attack, to ignore the narrative and appropriate the visual imagery to his or her own purposes, assuming, thereby, a belief in the primacy of the visual over the verbal as the preeminent means of communication. What the filmmaker might render banal, the spectator reanimates with a keen awareness of the "media echoes" to which the footage gives rise.

Lost in America

The road movie became an active genre in the late 1960s as the portability of lightweight camera equipment facilitated the process of taking the movies to the streets. Filmmakers, like their characters, went off in search of America, but all too often they made that quest without leaving their prejudices and preconceptions behind. Their sense of the divisions within the national consciousness uncritically incorporated well worn political and social stereotypes, resulting in a propensity for knee-jerk apocalypticism. Too many sixties films reflect "the American tendency to take the national pulse all the time, . . . skepticism and anxiety tend to outpace the mastery of fact. American life [becomes] a drag strip of hotted-up crises."

A choice example of the liability of uncritically exploring the national consciousness is *Easy Rider* (1969). For all the film's reputation as a historical landmark, its visual style owes a great deal to prior experimentation by its cinematographer, Laszlo Kovacs, who shot *Hell's Angels on Wheels* and *Psych-Out* among other exploitation features, and its plot reduces the characters to fashionably one-dimensional representatives of all-knowing hippies and know-nothing rednecks. Billy (Peter Fonda) and Wyatt's (Dennis Hopper) martyrdom seems undeserved, and Billy's ominous comment, "we blew it," implies a greater degree of self-consciousness than the duo's limited appreciation of their questionable behavior would allow. Stephan Farber highlights the film's deficiencies when he writes: "It's true that respectable America tends to stereotype the outsiders—hippies, radicals, blacks—and see them in conspiratorial terms; so why should we praise a hip-youth-oriented film that stereotypes its enemies just as ruthlessly, and also casts them as conspirators." Too many viewers of the film, one of the most financially successful in 1969, ignored the thematic deficiencies Farber underscored and reveled instead in its heroes' self-righteousness, often acted out at the expense of others, particularly rural Americans and women.

A far more telling, better modulated, and too little known road movie is Francis Ford Coppola's *The Rain People* (1969), in which Natalie (Shirley Knight), pregnant and feeling entrapped by her marriage, leaves home and takes to the freedom of the highways only to become burdened by the care of a brain-damaged, college football player, "Killer" Kilgannon (James Caan). Coppola, who shot the film over five months travelling from New York to Wyoming, captures the spaciousness of the landscape without losing track of the abominations brought about by our pillaging of the environment. Furthermore, he uses the road genre to tackle the issue of female liberation, although the narrative fluctuates between admiring and admonishing Natalie's quest for self-identity. Coppola cleverly highlights Natalie's habit of referring to herself in the third person and dramatizes her indecision during a series of long distance phone calls to her abandoned husband. Nonetheless, the conclusion opts for a facile tragedy and leaves Natalie cradling the now dead Killer, promising to protect him as she will likely protect the child she has deliberated over aborting earlier in the film. Coppola's film may not be politically correct, as he simultaneously promotes and discredits Natalie's liberation. Nonetheless, *The Rain People* is dramatically engrossing and too little known. By focusing on the admittedly incoherent narrative of female liberation, we can appreciate a precursor to more unified narratives.

Packaging Protest

The reflexive gesture toward a flip cynicism is particularly evident in the campus protest film cycle of 1970, typified by *The Strawberry Statement*, adapted from James S. Kunen's memoir of the Columbia uprising of 1968. It pits noble, good-looking, white, middle-class students against the retrograde entrenched forces of the establishment in such a manner that it virtually rewrites the teenpic in quasi-political terms: they could have called it *Beach Party Barricades*. One is unable to recontextualize these films as anything other than the cynical marketing of better riots with beautiful people. Despite Motion Picture Association of America President Jack Valenti's 1967 assertion "I truly don't think the entire young audience, and surely not the old, are all of a psychedelic breed, hunkered up over their pot and acid, and lurching off on supernatural romps and trips," the campus protest cycle proves Hollywood can and will package *anything.*

A representative example of this cycle is Richard Rush's *Getting Straight* (1970), one of several films released in that year starring Elliot Gould, who temporarily became an anti-authoritarian icon in the aftermath of *M*A*S*H* (1969). Set in a state institution that epitomizes the academic model of the "multiversity," designed by the University of California's Chancellor Clark Kerr, the film details the academic failure and re-radicalization of Harry Bailey, a former activist now master's candidate and hopeful secondary-school teacher. Harry attempts to balance his libido and liberal conscience, constantly racing between the classroom and the bedroom. As his campus boils over into a full-fledged riot, Harry evades solicitations from all sides to ally himself with any number of causes, each of which he puts off with sarcastic bravado. It is only when he fails his master's oral examination, brought down by a professor's vehement denunciation of Fitzgerald as a closet homosexual, and is reunited with his girlfriend, Jan (Candace Bergen), that Harry commits himself to radical action and joins the rioting students.

However, the priorities for which the students strike in *Getting Straight* lack any substance. Even Harry realizes this, for when a campus administrator attacks their behavior, Harry responds, "It has nothing to do with politics. It's personal identity." *Getting Straight*'s characterization of politics as a matter of pique, not principle, amounts to little more than asserting that it's one step from rallying for co-ed dorms to offing the pigs. This indecisiveness is paralleled by Rush's use of a photographic technique known as "rack focus." With it one changes or "racks" focus from foreground to background, blurring one space and then the other rather than changing camera position. The degree to which rack focus subverts depth in the image is comparable to Harry Bailey's inability to integrate his personal-sexual and political-social concerns. The optical lack of cohesion suggest that Rush, like his characters, cannot imagine the continual interdependence between individual and society, part and whole except through acts of unreasoning violence. . . .

A more legitimate and coherently conceived expression of the period's revolutionary tensions is the explicit agitprop political drama epitomized by Haskell Wexler's *Medium Cool* (1968). An imperfect but compelling work, it unfortunately has borne the weight of being the period's only studio-produced piece of political cinema that attempted to incorporate a fictional narrative, detailing the recognition by television cameraman John (Robert Foster) of his co-option by the powers that be, with documentary footage of a revolutionary crisis, the riots that occurred during the Chicago demonstrations of 1968. The film seamlessly, if self-consciously, shifts between narrative and documentary modes, particularly when it features Wexler's actual footage of the police riots, used here as Eileen (Verna Bloom) searches for her missing son. However, it too often heats up into indigestible propagandizing, as in the sequence shot at a roller derby, which leadenly comments on the American propensity for indiscriminate violence. Admittedly, other sequences, particularly those shot during the convention, are undeniably effective as when, one hears Wexler's offscreen soundman cry, "Look out Haskell. It's real," after the police drop tear gas cannisters into the crowd. However, it is the quieter moments, particularly those between John and Eileen's son Harold (Harold Blankenship) and the flashbacks to Harold's childhood in West Virginia, which resonate in one's memory. Early in the film, during a discussion by a roomful of newsmen over the scope of a reporter's responsibilities, John states, "Who wants to see someone sitting? Who wants to see someone lying down? Who wants to see someone talking peace unless they're talking loud?" While Wexler's film too often focuses on such moments of ideological aggression, the film can be recontextualized to argue for the validity and significance of recording just such quieter, domestic moments. If our political consciousness remains merely a set of self-dramatizing gestures that do not carry over to our quotidian behavior, then we are merely narcissistically engaging in self-aggrandizement.

Social Erosion

Finally, one of the most impressive and too little known documents of the social changes in the 1960s is Richard Lester's

Petulia (1968). Shot in San Francisco during the 1967 "summer of love," it was the first film that Lester, a native born American who has lived his adult life in England, shot in this country. It was also the occasion of his return after fifteen years abroad. Scorned upon its release, during the aftermath of Robert Kennedy's assassination, as a morally reprehensible chronicle of a set of unredeemable characters, this film makes, not only emotional, but also formal demands upon the viewer. Rather than playing to our reflexive stereotypes, Lester fragments the narrative, incorporating flashbacks and flashforwards which elicit, if not demand, the viewer's active participation in the narrative. Furthermore, while the narrative may seem only obliquely political, concerning as it does the lives of the leisure and professional class in San Francisco, *Petulia* is, nonetheless, one of the most telling documents of the period. It denies the period's predominant ethos, that love can solve all dilemmas, by dramatizing the casual violence that plagues our lives and eats away at appropriate relationships.

The leading characters in the film, surgeon Archie (George C. Scott) and Petulia (Julie Christie), struggle with their belief that individuals can provide one another a safe haven in a heartless world. "Touch it. Touch it. Make the hurt less," Petulia asks Archie as she suffers through labor at the end of the film. The image of touch, highlighted by Lester's frequent shots of Archie's surgeon's hands, is central to the film as Petulia is battered more than once by the hands of her beautiful but impotent husband, David (Richard Chamberlain). Petulia has married him because he was, she confesses, "the most perfect thing I'd ever met. . . . He must be one of those plastic gadgets the Americans make so well. But I want one." She has objectified her husband, and he has acted in kind by treating her as a beautiful accessory to his upper-class life, albeit one to be battered when it gets out of line. So too is the Mexican boy Oliver (Vincent Arias), who the couple take home with them, argue over, and then treat as an object of pity when he is injured in a car accident. These characters, rich as their material lives might be, are, as Lester states, "emotional eunuchs in a society so riddled with the cancer of its own failing that commitment is never made."

However, *Petulia* does not focus on these characters alone.

It mirrors their emotionally bankrupt lives by depicting San Francisco, circa 1967, as an environment in which a death wish pervades and eventually triumphs over the summer of love. Television sets are a ubiquitous presence in *Petulia*, always tuned to the news of the Vietnam War. Furthermore, random episodes of violence occupy the frame along with the major characters, creating an unsettling aura of incipient calamity. Even the young people, the denizens of the "summer of love," appear lost in a world of their own. As Petulia, battered by her husband, is carried to an ambulance, the crowd, which oddly includes members of the Grateful Dead, rubbernecks around the stretcher; "Bye, bye mama. Write if you get work," one of them sarcastically cries out.

While *Petulia* is an effective and emotionally devastating, bittersweet romance, the viewer can easily recontextualize the narrative into a prescient portrait of an eroding society. "Isn't it super. Suddenly all that love," Petulia says to Archie soon after they first meet. A comment one might read as comic, yet Lester sees the film as the farthest thing from a comedy; instead, it depicts "people [who] are aware of what's wrong and therefore not only have the problems of being, but the problems of knowing about being—the double agony." *Petulia* reminds us that a film need not exhaust, but can multiply, its own possibilities by making demands upon its viewers, not predigesting its meaning or relying upon uninformed stereotypes. It fulfills Lester's aim: "I want to offer the scattershot of experience to an audience and make them work. I want to make each person sitting in a row see a different film."

From Creative to Corporate

We presently live in a period where the cinema bears, not only a resemblance to the techniques of commercial advertising, but also acts as a shill for the very corporations that now own the major Hollywood studios. As Mark Crispin Miller has shown, the pervasive use of commercial films as platforms for "product placement" damages the very nature of film narrative, but more profoundly indicates a radical shift of creative power out of the hands of filmmaking professionals into those of the CEOs. And the quantitative mentality of the corporate mind holds little interest in ambiguity or critique. The result is "going to the movies now is about as memorable as going to the airport. Conceived and sold as 'product,' just like the many products that it sells, so does the movie pass right through you, leaving nothing in you but the vague, angry craving for another one."

Too many current films so fully exhaust their possibilities and ignore contradictions that a happy ending, devoid of irony, is a prerequisite; when and if audience research indicates displeasure with a less than buoyant conclusion which might damage a film's box-office potential, the narrative is modified to fulfill the spectators' demands. Such practices embody what Andrew Britton has called Reaganite entertainment, which he defines as that which "refers to itself in order to persuade us that it doesn't refer outwards at all. It is, purely and simply 'entertainment'—and we all know what *that* is." These films do not merely lack a personal point of view, but their producers seem more than willing to change their substance to suit an audience's needs and desires, a cynical gesture that erases the line between creation and marketing and assumes spectators to be little more than "drugged faceless consumer(s)." Yet worst of all, Britton suggests, even should a film imply that reality is intolerable, it eradicates any possibility of social transformation by asserting that reality is immutable and any desire to escape or transcend it is a flight of fantasy.

Such circumstances make the process of recontextualization ever more difficult, yet, in looking back at the films of the 1960s, one recognizes, for all their self-contradiction, potential models of alternate expression equally worthy of attention as the social movements they attempt to document.

Television Offers an Escape from the Troubled Times

Josh Ozersky

In 1968, a year defined by riots, assassinations, and war, the top ten television programs gave no hint that America was facing troubled times. As columnist Josh Ozersky notes in the following article, television programmers throughout the 1960s were still clinging to the conservative piety of the previous decade. Federal Communications Commission regulations forbade sex, violence, and disrespect for authority on TV, and therefore the social conflict being played out in America's streets in 1968 was never reflected in network programs other than the news. Instead, as Ozersky points out, the popular programs of the mid-to-late-1960s were zany comedies, Westerns, and variety shows, all of which offered an escape from cultural anxiety derived from the protest movement, civil rights marches, and the Vietnam War.

Although Ozersky utilizes several popular situation comedies to illustrate that escapism captured the mood of network programming, he focuses on *The Beverly Hillbillies* as exemplary of the trend. *The Beverly Hillbillies* uses as its backdrop the glamorous fantasy world of Beverly Hills, where street fighters, protesters, Vietnam veterans, and civil rights activists never strayed. There amid the greedy and callous society of the moneyed elite, the show deposits the Clampetts, a family of honest, plainspoken country

■

bumpkins. Ozersky claims that with this formula, *The Beverly Hillbillies* not only kept the real world at bay for viewers but also touched the audience's nostalgic pining for simpler times, traditional values, and personal integrity idealized by the Clampetts' untainted worldview and salt-of-the-earth morality.

Ozersky therefore acknowledges that while much of the escapist fantasy was foisted upon American TV viewers, it was not always unwelcome by those living through the decade's social upheaval. Still, no decade of television since the 1960s has been so obviously divorced from its social and political environment. Starting in the 1970s, the baby boomers—the force of change in the 1960s—would come to demand more realism in television, even in their situation comedies.

Josh Ozersky writes on cultural history. His articles have appeared in such publications as *Newsday* and the *Washington Post*.

FEW THINGS ARE MORE STRIKING, IN RETRO-spect, than the sheer obliviousness of prime-time television in 1968 to the turmoil surrounding it in the real world. Cataclysm followed cataclysm on the news. January brought the Tet offensive [in which North Vietnamese soldiers and South Vietnamese guerrilla forces attacked major cities deep in the heart of South Vietnam], an astonishing rebuttal to official reassurances about the Vietnam War. So discouraging was this news that, in an unprecedented act, news anchor Walter Cronkite himself was prompted to break with all tradition and suggest, onscreen and *ex cathedra*, that the war might be unwinnable. "We are mired in stalemate," Cronkite pronounced, ". . . the only rational way out [is] . . . to negotiate not as victors, but as an honorable people who lived up to their pledge to defend democracy and did the best they could." (President Johnson, watching on one of his three TVs, immediately turned to his press secretary to say that he had now lost Mr. Average Citizen.) April brought the death of Martin Luther King Jr., and summer, the death of Robert Kennedy; each event was the occasion of immense television coverage, as well as violent social and political aftershocks. Summer also brought the infamous Chicago Democratic Convention, where such deathless images were generated as Dan Rather being wrestled to the ground and Mayor Daley's police brutalizing protesters. These were defining moments in TV's history (they would later become universal signifiers of "the sixties" for lazy producers); moreover, they were far from isolated spectacles in 1968. The occupation of universities, most notably Columbia, by student radicals; President Johnson's announcement that he would not run again; and most of all, the endless procession of depressing or inflammatory images from the war flooded millions of American living rooms with discord, violence, and ominous instability.

In prime time, however, the shows listed in table 1.1 were rated in the A.C. Nielsen Company's top ten as of April 1968. (*The Saturday Movie of the Week*, which would occupy eighth place, is omitted). The proverbial viewer from outer space, receiving these broadcasts a billion years hence in his recliner in the Crab Nebula, would infer from them only the most ephemeral of social problems. They consisted of three pastoral comedies, two Westerns, a liver-spotted handful of aging-star vehicles, and a pair of ludicrous sitcoms—one about two cute children in the care of an English valet, and the other about a housewife with magic powers.

Table 1.1 Top Ten Shows, 1968

Program/Network	Rating
1. *The Andy Griffith Show*, CBS	31.8
2. *The Lucy Show*, CBS	27.0
3. *Gunsmoke*, CBS	25.6
4. *Family Affair*, CBS	25.5
5. *Bonanza*, NBC	25.5
6. *The Red Skelton Show*, CBS	25.5
7. *The Dean Martin Show*, CBS	24.8
8. *The Jackie Gleason Show*, CBS	23.9
9. *Bewitched*, CBS	23.5
10. *The Beverly Hillbillies*, CBS	23.3

Only in historical retrospect, however, do the Nielsen top ten look so irrelevant. For the networks, they were relevant indeed, because in 1968, as now, what mattered most to TV executives was the getting and the keeping of highly rated shows.

And since the audience was seen for the most part as an undifferentiated mass, the idea of airing polarizing material, which at that time any genuinely realistic show would necessarily have been, simply ran against the grain of network thinking.

Clinging to a Conservative Code

Television, it will be remembered, was very much a product of the 1950s. Although the primness of *The Adventures of Ozzie and Harriet* (1952–1966) had gone the way of vaudeville, the industry's moral principles circa 1950 were never repudiated. In 1967, for example, the National Association of Broadcasters revised their Television Code for the twelfth time. Though widely regarded within the industry as an absurd and unenforceable document, it still served as the NAB's official conscience. Meant to be applied "to every moment of every program presented by television," its first article read, "Commercial television provides a valuable means of augmenting the educational and cultural influence of schools, institutions of higher learning, the home, the church, museums, foundations, and other institutions of education and culture." Among its commandments were:

> 5. Attacks on religion and religious faiths are not allowed. Reverence is to mark any mention of the name of God, His attributes and powers. . . . The office of minister, priest, or rabbi shall not be presented in such a manner as to ridicule or impair its dignity. . . .

> 9. Law enforcement shall be upheld and, except where essential to the program plot, officers of the law portrayed with respect and dignity. . . .

> 16. Illicit sex relations are not treated as commendable. Sex crimes and abnormalities are generally unacceptable as program material. The use of locations closely associated with sexual life or with sexual sin must be governed by good taste and delicacy.

> 17. Drunkenness should never be presented as desirable or prevalent. The use of liquor in program content shall be deemphasized. The consumption of liquor in American life, when not required by the plot or for proper characterization, shall not be shown.

Other injunctions against impropriety, lewdness, disrespect for authority, hypnosis, astrology, and "the use of horror for its own sake" were also included among the code's pie-in-the-sky restrictions.

It was, in short, a puritanical and wholly abstract document, bearing almost as little relation to TV circa 1968 as TV did to reality. What is significant is that even at this late date such lip-service to the civic pietism of the Eisenhower era was felt necessary and proper. Part of this was a reaction to criticism in the public sector and also in government that persisted long after the departure of President Kennedy's much-hated FCC chairman Newton Minow in 1964 and in fact persists to this day. Minow had railed against TV as a "vast wasteland" and threatened to revoke broadcast licenses unless the networks took responsibility. In 1968, Senator John Pastore (D-Rhode Island) began a campaign against TV violence. In such situations, the broadcast industry tended to wrap itself in civic-minded pronouncements of similar spirit to the code, often made by its statesmen, like President Frank Stanton of CBS. In 1968, in the wake of the Kennedy and King assassinations, the networks hastened to demonstrate the seriousness with which they took the senator's concern by sending notice to producers that violence had to be toned down. Aware that the heat must eventually pass, the producers and programmers obliged by reducing almost to nil the stylized shootings and fisticuffs that had filled so much of the airtime of Westerns and police dramas. A policeman might shoot a fleeing criminal and then inexplicably go over to him to confirm that he was still alive. As television historians Harry Castleman and Walter Podzarik note, "These strange new rules and illogical twists for action stories gave the 1968–1969 season the derogatory nickname of 'the one punch season.'". . .

Nostalgia for Down-Home Values

The status quo rules in television. And beyond this, the fact is that television's bottomless appetite for programming requires far more scripts, pilots, projects, and productions than can possibly be made with any sort of wit or intelligence. Then as now, TV shows were ground out with the uniformity of sausage links, and few writers in any case had any control over their work. Nearly all scripts were vetted by producers, directors, and executives with the care of a bishop examining a new catechism for hints of heterodoxy. Quality was not a high priority. "The shocking thing," said writer Ray Bradbury in 1967, "is that TV doesn't really want fine material."

What kind of material, then, did TV want? To judge by the top ten Nielsen shows (for this was surely how the networks judged the issue), the stress was on a kind of burnished escapism. Producers had a vague idea that most of their audience was rural—and that, in any case, urban viewers were more likely to enjoy a rural show than the other way around. . . .

For CBS in the 1960s, the ideal, if not the reality, of rural America, [held] sway. And if there was any doubt, it was dispelled by the very biggest hit of the decade, *The Beverly Hillbillies*, which began a phenomenal sitcom run in 1962.

No sitcom, not even *I Love Lucy*, had ascended to the heights of the ratings in so short a time—six weeks. No sitcom was ever so roundly despised by critics upon its inception (David Susskind even asked his viewers to write to Congress in protest), thus proving yet again how irrelevant "the eggheads" were to popular tastes.

The basic premise of the show was, as they say, as old as the hills. Ozark mountain folk [the Clampett family], after striking oil, find themselves living among the decadent rich in Beverly Hills. Hilarity ensues, as *TV Guide* might say. But in the case of *The Beverly Hillbillies*, concept was not all. *The Beverly Hillbillies* represented a departure from the current fashions in situation comedy. The sitcom, although divested of its all-knowing Dad and zero-sum suburban "adventures," in 1962 still relied on domestic settings, "normal" families, and at least the accoutrements of realism. . . .

The Beverly Hillbillies looked different than other sitcoms. Starkly artificial and stylized, it brought an element of theatricality to what had become an increasingly sterile genre. The characters were highly individuated but at the same time highly artificial and formalized, owing more to the stage and its iconic costuming than to the B-feature conventions of most filmed series. [Beverly Hills banker] Mr. Drysdale is always wearing a different Brooks Brothers suit, and playboy Dash Riprock the era's flashy sportswear, but the Clampetts are always dressed exactly the same: Jed's torn felt hat, Jethro's rope belt and red plaid shirts, Granny's high-collared blouse. Like the Chinaman's pigtail or the Blimp's monocle, these are traditional identity tags of the kind familiar to stage audiences. (As amazing as it seems today, most suburban sitcoms of the 1950s were meant to seem realistic, not eerie and otherworldly as we regard them today.) *The Beverly Hillbillies'* artificiality inflamed critics still enamored of the realism of *Playhouse 90* (1956–1961), *Omnibus* (1953–1957), and the "golden age" of live drama. "Their assorted adventures," wrote the *New York Times*, "don't merely strain credulity, they crush it" But to audiences, the show's fantastic element was liberating.

There was also a historical element to *The Beverly Hillbillies'* success. By the late 1950s, a critical literature had begun to accrue around the perceived consumerism and materialism of the postwar years. As it became clear that the economic perils of the 1930s and 1940s seemed to be safely behind, a kind of cottage industry developed. A large popular bibliography could be assembled from the mid-to-late 1950s of nonpartisan works that lamented the disappearance of American virtues. John Keats's *The Crack in the Picture Window* (1957) and *The Insolent Chariots* (1959) attacked the pursuit of homes and cars upon which so much of the postwar economic boom rested. Vance Packard's *The Hidden Persuaders* (1957) and *The Status Seekers* (1959) attacked advertising and consumerism, respectively, to wide attention and applause; the charismatic sociologist C. Wright Mills published several books, including *White Collar* (1951) and *The Power Elite* (1956), which were both class analyses of America with more than a little jeremiad in them. Novelist John Steinbeck, in a *New Republic* essay titled "Have We Gone Soft?" summed up the theme best: "If I wanted to destroy a nation, I would give it too much and I would have it on its knees, miserable, greedy, and sick. . . . On all levels American society is rigged. . . . I am troubled by the cynical immorality of my country. It cannot survive on this basis." Most of these books, essays, speeches, and discussion were predicated, in one way or another, on the notion that Americans have declined from the virtues, Spartan and otherwise, of the forefathers. . . .

It would be ludicrous to say that *The Beverly Hillbillies* shared the target audience of these high- and middlebrow critiques, but it clearly shares a longing for the world we have lost. "Jed Clampett was to be a tall man of simple, homespun honesty and dignity," Paul Henning, the show's creator, told the press upon its premiere. "The kind of Ozark mountaineer I knew as a boy." This remark suggests an added appeal of the show, besides its use as a pastoral for the affluent society. Jed Clampett and his family are meant to represent pure American types, the sort of people Paul Henning remembered from his boyhood in Independence, Missouri, where as a soda jerk he served up phosphates to Harry S. Truman. . . .

Escapism Pays Off

As the world around it became increasingly bewildering and hostile, [cultural critic Eric] Barnouw suggests, TV became a "psychological refuge" for the "average man's view of the world. . . . It presented the America he wanted and believed in and had labored to be part of. It was alive with handsome men and women and symbols of the good life. It invited and drew him into its charmed circle." Whether or not this was the case is impossible to say; Barnouw is extrapolating as all observers must from the Nielsen ratings and the character of the day's programming.

That having been said, Barnouw's point is well taken. By a kind of Darwinian trial and error, the networks in the early 1960s had discovered that escapism paid off. Throughout the decade, CBS president James Aubrey oversaw the development of feather-light entertainments, which he felt were the strength of CBS's winning prime-time lineup. In some cases, this meant rural escapism, slavish knock-offs of *The Beverly Hillbillies'* winning formula. In Paul Henning's *Green Acres* (1965–1971), the formula is simply reversed: two high-society types, counterparts to the Drysdales, move out to "Hooterville," where they get caught up in culture shock and rural high jinks. . . .

Although the rural sitcoms could not replicate themselves indefinitely (subgenres, as a rule, bearing small litters), their escapist spirit came to dominate the decade. Although only a few actually had rural settings, all represented the kind of pastoral tranquility the countryside represented to the TV networks, or at least to their directing intelligences on the four-hundredth floor of the corporate headquarters in Manhattan. As Harry Castleman and Walter Podzarik put it, "the aseptic peace of Fifties TV had been transported to the hills and nothing could disturb it."

Thus, as the Vietnam War escalated, for example, audiences were treated to an odd subgenre of bloodless, playful war comedies: *Gomer Pyle, U.S.M.C.* (1964–1970), in which a dim-witted gas station attendant from Andy Griffith's hometown, inducted into the marines, clashes week after week with his crusty but benevolent drill instructor and a swell bunch of barrack mates who have never heard of Vietnam; *Hogan's Heroes* (1965–1971), in which a motley group of POWs operate an undercover operation under the nose of bumbling Colonel Klink; *McHale's Navy* (1962–1966), in which Ernest Borgnine and his PT crew had zany adventures outwitting their commanding officer in the Pacific theater of World War II; and *The Wackiest Ship in the Army* (1965–1966), about the nutty crew of a two-masted schooner in World War II who, as Ed Papazian memorably puts it, "halted the merriment from time to time to gun down hordes of comic book 'Japs' who made the mistake of getting in their way." Long-running Westerns like *Bonanza* (1959–1973) and *Gunsmoke* (1955–1975) and star-powered variety institutions like *The Ed Sullivan Show* (1945–1971) and Jack Benny's *Collegiate Comedy Hour* (1950–1965) helped to round out the Nielsens through the early and mid-1960s, with occasional police or medical dramas thrown in for good measure.

If such diversions, aired in the years of escalation (the Tonkin Gulf resolution coming in 1964, Operation Rolling Thunder and the first combat troops in 1965) represented a pointed escapism, a comedy of containment, the suburban sitcoms of this period evidenced an even more legible desperation. The *Ozzie and Harriet* model having played itself out, programmers in search of nonconfrontational suburban comedies turned to the fantastic. This became apparent by the 1964 season. Then, as Castleman and Podzarik put it, "in contrast to the fondly remembered high drama of TV's golden days, the networks' fall schedules offered country bumpkins, ridiculous settings, childish plots, witches, Martians, and pure soap opera. It all seemed deliberately designed to appeal to viewers who looked at television as a mindless escape tool."

Television News Brings the Vietnam War Home

Chester J. Pach Jr.

The Vietnam War was the first conflict in American history to be televised and broadcast into homes across the nation. Images of jungle grass, helicopters, and occasional firefights became standard fare for families congregated around the dinner table. Undoubtedly, the televised portrait of Vietnam shaped viewers' opinions of the war as it progressed, but it is not clear how or to what degree. Some historians have attributed the public's growing dissatisfaction with America's involvement in Vietnam in part to the way in which television used combat footage and sensationalistic images to cover the conflict. In the following article, Chester J. Pach Jr., an associate professor of history at Ohio University, disputes this cause and effect notion as simplistic.

Instead of merely blaming the media's sensational imagery as a cause for the nation's discontent, Pach examines the war from the broadcasters' perspective. According to Pach, the television journalists in Vietnam wanted to concentrate on covering battlefield operations because they believed that mothers and fathers in America wanted to see what their sons were doing and where they were likely to be. But obtaining battlefield footage was difficult and dangerous, so little of it was actually aired. Instead, television reporters devoted their time to human interest stories

■

Chester J. Pach Jr., "And That's the Way It Was: The Vietnam War on the Network Nightly News," *The Sixties: From Memory to History*, edited by David Farber. Chapel Hill: University of North Carolina Press, 1994. Copyright © 1994 by University of North Carolina Press. All rights reserved. Reproduced by permission.

and profiles of combat soldiers. Because of limited airtime, though, both the human interest pieces and the combat footage flew by with little media analysis, leaving viewers with disjointed images of often terrified and tired soldiers and hectic firefights. Ironically, according to Pach, these fragmentary images accurately reflected the nature of the war, which was itself confusing and incoherent. Thus the media unwittingly captured the war as it actually was.

"AS I SAT IN MY OFFICE LAST EVENING, WAITING to speak," Lyndon B. Johnson told the National Association of Broadcasters on 1 April 1968, the day after he announced he would not seek another term as president, "I thought of the many times each week when television brings the [Vietnam] war into the American home." What Americans saw each night in their living room, Johnson believed, was a distorted picture of the war, one dominated by "dramatic" events, such as the spectacular but temporary enemy successes during the recent Tet Offensive [when North Vietnamese troops and South Vietnamese guerrillas attacked major cities throughout South Vietnam]. Johnson conceded that it was impossible to determine exactly how "those vivid scenes" had shaped popular attitudes. He also acknowledged that "historians must only guess at the effect that television would have had . . . during the Korean war, . . . when our forces were pushed back there to Pusan" or during World War II when the Germans counterattacked at the Battle of the Bulge. Still, Johnson suggested that it was no accident that previous administrations had weathered these military reverses, but his had suffered a debilitating loss of popular support during the Tet Offensive. The reason for the "very deep and very emotional divisions" in public opinion was that Vietnam was America's first televised war.

Johnson was one of many who have criticized, albeit for different reasons, TV coverage of the Vietnam War. Like Johnson, some observers have faulted television for oversimplifying the complexities of Vietnam or for emphasizing spectacular, but horrifying scenes of combat that shocked viewers into opposing the war. In contrast, other commentators have denounced TV journalists for all too easily accepting official pronouncements of progress, at least until Tet, or for making the war's brutality seem so stylized, trivialized, or routine that the result was acceptance or ennui rather than revulsion. Many scholars have argued that television news came of age during Vietnam, although one influential critic has insisted that fundamental weaknesses in American journalism produced a distorted assessment of the Tet Offensive as an American failure. The most extreme critics blame television for reporting so ignorant, biased, or deceptive that it turned the victory American soldiers had won on the battlefields of Vietnam into defeat by producing irresistible political pressures for withdrawal.

Television, however, did better at covering the war than many of these critics allow. To be sure, television's view of the war was limited, usually to what the camera could illustrate with vivid images. Too many film reports on the network newscasts dealt with American military operations, and too often they concentrated on immediate events—a firefight or an air strike—with little, if any, analysis of how those incidents fit into larger patterns of the war. Yet television also showed the war as it was—a confused, fragmented, and questionable endeavor. Brief reports, usually no more than three minutes long, of isolated, disconnected military engagements, broadcast night after night, week after week, magnified the confusing features of a war that, at best, was hard to fathom—one usually without fronts, clearly identifiable enemies, reliable progress toward victory, or solid connections to American security. Because of the nature of the medium rather than any conscious effort, television nightly news exposed the irrationalities of a war that lacked coherent strategy or clear purpose.

Relations Between the Press and the White House

When Johnson decided in 1965 to send American combat troops to Vietnam, TV journalists faced a unique challenge. Vietnam was television's first war. The three major networks rapidly enlarged their operations in Vietnam and by 1967 were each spending over $1 million annually on covering the war. The expansion of the nightly newscasts on CBS and NBC from fifteen to thirty minutes in September 1963—ABC did not follow suit until January 1967—provided more time for Vietnam news. The state of broadcast technology, however, made for substantial delays in airing stories from Vietnam. Not until February 1967 was it possible to relay film by satellite from Tokyo to New York, but then only at a cost of as much as $5,000 for a five-minute transmission. Thus all but the most urgent stories continued to be flown from Saigon to New York for broadcasting. Television viewers usually learned about the most recent developments in Vietnam from the anchor's summary of wire service copy. They commonly had to wait another two days to see film reports of those events.

Unlike those who covered World War II or Korea, Vietnam correspondents did not have military censors review their reports, but they did face informal restrictions and pressures. Johnson was obsessed with the news—"television and radio were his constant companions," wrote one biographer [Doris Kearns]—and he was determined to get reporters to promote his version of the national interest. "I'm the only president you've got, and . . . I need your help," he told members of the White House press corps. But if they did not cooperate, Johnson warned them, "I know how to play it both ways, too." Like Johnson, public information officers for the U.S. command in Vietnam tried to use informal pressures to shape reporting on Vietnam. They rejected censorship because they doubted its effectiveness and feared that it would anger correspondents. Instead, they outlined a series of guidelines that restricted identification of specific units or disclosure of the exact number of casualties in individual battles. They relied on daily news briefings, derisively known as the "Five O'Clock Follies," to influence the coverage of military operations. And they hoped that a vast array of incentives—transportation on military aircraft, interviews with commanders, lodging at bases—would secure or maintain a good working relationship with correspondents and thus favorable coverage of the war effort.

The War of Attrition

The war that these reporters covered had a superficial, but ultimately specious logic. In South Vietnam, U.S. ground forces tried to win the war with a strategy of attrition. Their primary mission was to search out and destroy the main units of the Vietcong and the North Vietnamese army. The U.S. commander, General William C. Westmoreland, insisted that wearing down these conventional forces had to take precedence over rooting out guerrillas from populated areas. . . . Westmoreland's strategy of attrition, according to Earle Wheeler, the chairman of the Joint Chiefs of Staff, provided "the best assurance of military victory in South Vietnam."

Despite Wheeler's assertion, the strategy of attrition utterly failed. The big battles that Westmoreland sought occurred only infrequently. Instead, by 1967 Vietnam had become a small-unit war in which 96 percent of the engagements involved an enemy force no larger than a company (150 soldiers). These battles usually took place only when the enemy chose to fight. By seizing the initiative, the North Vietnamese and the Vietcong were able to control their casualties and frustrate the strategy of attrition. . . .

Attrition proved to be, at best, an incoherent strategy, at worst, no strategy at all. A study ordered by the army's chief of staff found that there was "no unified effective pattern" to U.S. military operations. Troops in the field reached the same conclusion through hard experience. The lack of front lines or territorial objectives made them frustrated and cynical. "Without a front, flanks, or rear, we fought a formless war against a formless enemy who evaporated like the morning jungle mists, only to materialize in some unexpected place," recalled Philip Caputo, a marine officer who saw action in 1965–66. . . .

What Viewers Saw

On television, the most important story about Vietnam was the fighting that involved U.S. forces. About half of the film reports on network newscasts concerned U.S. troops on foot or in helicopters searching out the enemy, exchanging fire with snipers, calling in air strikes on base camps and supply depots, or clearing guerrillas from hostile villages. (This "bang, bang" coverage crowded out stories about pacification or the inefficiencies of the South Vietnamese government, reports that would have provided viewers a deeper understanding of the complexities of counterinsurgency warfare.) Yet TV journalists thought that they were giving their audience the news it wanted. "There are approximately 500,000 American men

The Moon Landing: Spectacle in Space

Millions of Americans watched as Apollo 11's Eagle *module touched down on the moon's surface on July 20, 1969. It was a culturally defining moment for the nation, but it was also, as writer and radio commentator Steven D. Stark explains, a perfect example of televised spectacle.*

"People have the audacity to say nothing new is going on these days," [CBS news anchor Walter] Cronkite editorialized on the air during the moon mission in July 1969, a period when CBS, like NBC, was on the air for 30 hours straight. "I'd like to know what these kids are saying who pooh-poohed this. How can one turn off from a world like this?" It may have been how many Americans felt at the time, and Cronkite may have been close to setting records by being on the air for something over 17 hours straight. Still, it was unusual behavior for an anchor, conduct which revealed how this type of news coverage differed from anything else. Perhaps we might best think of it as being rather like the way that announcers present the Olympics today.

To cap things off for the moon mission, ABC commissioned Duke Ellington to write a new piece of music; NBC countered with James Earl Jones and Rod McKuen reading poetry; and CBS featured [architect and critic] Buckminster Fuller and Buster Crabbe (star of the old movie serial *Buck Rogers*). Thus, when the *Eagle* finally landed at 4:17 P.M. on that stellar Sunday, it seemed to some almost anticlimactic. This was truly the origin of news as stage production: Politicians would take note, and learn to drench their appearances in imagery and music based on what they had seen here.

Steven D. Stark, *Glued to the Set: The 60 Television Shows and Events That Made Us Who We Are Today.* New York: Free Press, 1997, pp. 105–106.

there," one reporter [Leonard Zeidenberg] explained. "When this is multiplied by parents, friends and other relatives, there is no doubt what is of most importance to Americans." TV journalists also believed that they were using their visual medium to best advantage. "The sensationalism in Vietnam is obviously in the combat," remarked one network reporter [Daniel C. Hallin]. "Editors want combat footage. They will give it good play.". . .

Such footage, however, was rare. Despite its potential to "describe in excruciating, harrowing detail what war is all about," the television camera only infrequently did so. Obtaining combat film was difficult; the television crew had to get out to the field, be lucky enough to accompany a unit that made contact with the enemy, and make sure that its equipment worked properly. "Then, if the battle is fierce," noted NBC's John Paxton, "the cameraman does not get the film because he usually has his face in the dirt."

If the camera operator did film the action, though, it might not be aired. In Saigon and Washington, military authorities cautioned television journalists that networks that showed objectionable scenes of American casualties might have their reporters barred from combat zones. Because of these warnings or their own scruples, editors hardly ever allowed ghastly pictures of the dead or dying into American homes during the dinner hour. Indeed, just 3 percent of news reports from Vietnam showed heavy fighting. . . .

Instead, television provided only suggestive glimpses of the war. Typical was a report by Morley Safer on 17 November 1965 from the attack troop ship *Paul Revere*, which was carrying marines to beaches south of Danang to begin a search-and-destroy mission. Safer's film captured the anticipation of combat, but none of the fighting. . . .

Often television focused not on battles but on the Americans who fought them. Human interest features reflected television's tendency to entertain as well as inform. A personalized story, TV journalists believed, appealed to their mass audience, perhaps because it often simplified—or avoided—complex or controversial issues. A staple of network newscasts was the combat interview, either with a commander or a hero. NBC's George Page, for example, reported in May 1967 from the Mekong Delta, where he talked to soldiers in the Ninth Infantry Division whose bravery had saved the lives of their comrades. Several days later, the "CBS Evening News" carried an interview that correspondent Mike Wallace had conducted with Lieutenant Colonel Robert Schweitzer, who had been wounded eight times and decorated on eleven occasions. . . . Occasionally newsworthy were the lives of ordinary soldiers away from battle, as when Safer interviewed a group on rest and recreation traveling to Hong Kong to catch up, they said, on sleeping, letter writing, and drinking "good homogenized milk.". . .

Lack of Media Analysts

Interpreting the war news was difficult, and television reporters often failed to provide analysis or commentary. The anchors of the nightly newscasts—Walter Cronkite on CBS, Chet Huntley and David Brinkley on NBC, and, successively, Peter Jennings, Bob Young, Frank Reynolds, and Howard K. Smith on ABC—offered no interpretation in more than half of the stories that they read. Their reticence was a result of their role in the program, which was to read short news items or introduce correspondents' reports. Less than one-fifth of their stories exceeded seventy-five words, which left little room for analytical comments. The canons of objective journalism—accuracy, balance, fairness, impartiality—also encouraged anchors to limit interpretive remarks. So too did the importance of inspiring confidence and loyalty among viewers, who often chose which network newscast to watch on the basis of their reaction to the personal qualities of the anchor. Walter Cronkite did not earn his reputation as the most trusted man in America by making partisan, gratuitous, or controversial comments about the news, but by reporting it "the way it was."

Network correspondents also did not supply much analysis in many of their stories about the war. Again, time limitations affected the content of their reports. With just twenty-two minutes each weekday night to present the news—commercials took up the rest of the half-hour program—television functioned as an electronic front page, covering little more than the day's most important occurrences, often in spare summaries. Correspondents' reports almost never ran more than three minutes and often considerably less. Television's preoccupation with the immediate—today's news—severely limited analytical reports intended to provide perspective. . . .

Yet television journalists did try to make sense of the war, frequently by comparing current military operations with previous ones. Measuring the size, scope, or cost of a military action was a convenient, albeit simplistic, way of assessing its importance. Network correspondents and anchors, for example, described the Battle of the Ia Drang Valley as the "biggest engagement yet," the "bloodiest, longest" battle since Korea, "classic infantry warfare," and "the biggest American victory yet in Vietnam.". . .

Television reporters also tried to understand current military events by speculating about their relationship with future developments in the war. Reasoning by extrapolation—projecting what happened today into next week or next month—was an easy, if risky, way of simplifying the complexities of Vietnam. Cronkite, for example, declared that the Battle of the Ia Drang Valley was a portent of "dramatic change" in the Vietnam War, while [reporter] Dean Brelis considered it a harbinger of more big battles. Yet staggering losses encouraged the North Vietnamese to avoid major engagements after Ia Drang and utilize guerrilla tactics instead. One year later, Cronkite predicted that a series of North Vietnamese and Vietcong military initiatives "could set the pattern of the war for months to come." But the anticipated major offensive did not occur. . . . However logical or appealing to television journalists, extrapolation clearly was a dubious method of discerning the future in Vietnam.

Much of the information and many of the interpretive comments in television newscasts prior to the Tet Offensive suggested that the United States was winning the war. When TV journalists assessed the results of battles during 1965–67, they concluded that about two-thirds were American victories. . . . From time to time military officials appeared in news reports to assure the public that American troops were achieving their goals, as when General John Deane told Page in November 1966 that the war was going "very well.". . .

Television Stands Behind Washington

The favorable treatment of the war effort reflected television's acceptance of the cold war outlook that was responsible for

U.S. intervention in Vietnam. TV journalists did not challenge President Johnson's conviction that the national interest required the containment of communism or the president's decision to commit U.S. combat troops to Vietnam. Those policies had such strong, mainstream support in 1965 that the network newscasts did not present them as matters of legitimate controversy. Instead, TV journalists responded to Johnson's decision to go to war in Vietnam less as objective journalists than as patriotic citizens. They reported the war effort in language that revealed a lack of detachment. Commonly in 1965–66, they referred to "our" troops, planes, and losses in Vietnam. The North Vietnamese or Vietcong were usually the "enemy," frequently the "Communists," and occasionally the "Reds.". . .

There were several reasons why the network newscasts seemed [in the words of Eric Barnouw] "to express a massive political consensus" at the beginning of the Vietnam War. Dependent on advertising revenues, subject to federal regulation, and vulnerable to pressure from affiliates, television networks were wary of controversial programming or discordant opinions. When J. William Fulbright (D-Ark.), the chair of the Senate Foreign Relations Committee, held hearings in February 1966 that disputed the Johnson administration's Vietnam policies, CBS broke off its coverage in favor of reruns of "I Love Lucy," "The Real McCoys," and "The Andy Griffith Show." Network executives cited neither commercial nor ideological reasons for their decision, but—fantastically—the danger that extended telecasting of the hearings would "obfuscate" or "confuse" the issues about the war. . . .

Such episodes have persuaded many observers that television in the mid-1960s was "the most timid" of the news media, the most willing to accept official statements at face value, the most reluctant to air dissenting opinions, the most likely to knuckle under to government pressure. . . . The news media in general seems to have shared dominant core values that made it inclined in 1965–66 to support—or, at least, not to question—the fundamental reasons for American intervention in Vietnam.

Television may have expressed those consensual values in unique or distinctive ways because network newscasts were not simply a source of information but also of entertainment. As

media analyst Peter Braestrup has argued, the
work correspondent in Vietnam "was not to p
the sense of 'fact-finding' . . . , but to obtain an
vignettes" that were "presented as 'typical' or a
the entire war. The correspondents who subm
reports often had only the most rudimentary
Vietnamese politics and culture, since their
ments usually lasted between six months and on
pertise was not in Southeast Asian affairs or
tional relations, but in producing vivid, engagi
stories. Even more than the correspondents,
producers in New York who assembled the
were masters not of interpreting the news but
Their concern was good television—reports fr
provided spectacular images that would attrac
and somehow encapsulate the entire war eff
minute segment. This was neither adversaria
analytical journalism. Instead, it was theatrica
flection of the nature of the expertise of televis

The Fragmented TV War Mirro Real War

What kind of war, then, did a television vie
network nightly news during the American
nam from 1965 through 1967? He or she sa
Arlen has remarked, a "generally distanced
jointed conflict which was composed mainly
copters landing, tall grasses blowing in th
American soldiers fanning out across a hill
at the ready, with now and then (on the so
ping or two, and now and then (as the vis
column of dark, billowing smoke a half mi
described as a burning Vietcong ammo d
night the American people peered at the
from a war that had been domesticated by
war was always there on the screen, close
or repel but not so close as to spoil dinner.
tles ended in American victories, althoug
revealed problems that suggested that all
Rarely, though, could the viewer see bey

Television's war was a series of disconnected episodes of combat. Television reporters usually did not look for the connections, but when they did, they had trouble finding them. That was because the strategy of attrition had produced a war of isolated engagements. The fragmented war on television was precisely the war fought in Vietnam. . . .

Did it matter that the Vietnam War was covered on television? How did TV reporting affect public attitudes toward the war? These are important questions, but they cannot be answered as precisely as we might wish. Television did affect public understanding of the war, since by 1970 a majority of Americans got most of their news from television. Yet what they learned from nightly newscasts is by no means clear. Studies have revealed that most viewers have trouble remembering anything from news programs that they just finished watching. Perhaps that is because, as one scholar [Lawrence Lichty] has observed, television "is designed to be watched intermittently, casually, and without full concentration. Only the commercials command and dazzle." Even if one does watch intently, the meaning one extracts from a news report is a product of individual values and attitudes. . . .

Yet even if it cannot be precisely measured, television's influence during the Vietnam War was important. Images do have powerful effects, however much the reaction varies among individual viewers. . . .

Television presented a war that was puzzling and incoherent—a series of disjointed military operations that were often individually successful but collectively, disastrous. Night after night, television slowly exposed the illogic of attrition. If viewers grew weary or discontent or outraged, it was partly because television just happened to show them an important part of the Vietnam War "the way it was."

3

EXAMINING POP CULTURE

Music and the Counterculture

The Hippies
Reject Mainstream
America

Terry H. Anderson

Terry H. Anderson is a professor of history at Texas
A&M University who has written extensively on the
1960s and the Vietnam War. In the following excerpt
from his book on the political protest movement of
the 1960s, Anderson narrates the advent of the hippies by infusing his own analysis with the words of
those who lived through the movement. According to
Anderson, the hippies were unlike the decade's "first
wave" of political activists, who were rather straight-
laced college students, intellectuals, and civil rights
advocates born in the 1930s and 1940s. These early
radicals took part in protests, formed organizations,
and exposed the wrongheaded policies of the nation.
The "second wave," in Anderson's terms, only
reached college during the mid-1960s. They had already inculcated the alternative ideals of the first
wave and therefore were less prone to organize and
debate. Instead, the second wave spawned, among
other groups, the hippies, an amorphous term that
applied to almost anyone who believed in the preach-
ing of the early activists but usually found less-
confrontational ways to show their allegiance to re-
making the nation.

The hippies generally advocated love over war,
peaceful coexistence over political hostility. Some hippies were still politically active; others were soured by

the seeming ineffectuality of the movement and re-treated to set up communes and other private enclaves where the ethics of peace, love, and acceptance might survive in a fracturing nation. As Anderson notes, the hippies sported specific clothes and hairstyles that clashed with those of the mainstream to denote their membership in the ill-defined counterculture. They experimented with drugs for pleasure and to escape the turmoil of the day. In short, they did everything they could to distance themselves from what they saw as the commercialistic and militaristic attitudes of mainstream America at the time. Yet as many critics including Anderson have pointed out, the hippie movement became so broad that many young people in the country claimed some piece of its ethics, music, or fashion without leaving the comfort of their main-stream lives. The movement eventually devolved, and its death was signaled when corporate America began marketing the image as trendy.

"HIPPIE," OF COURSE, OFTEN MEANT DIFFERENT things to the older and younger generations. Parents usually stated that hippies included everyone revolting against some-thing, or simply revolting to them, and mainstream journalists simply labeled them "dirty, costumed protesters" who had long hair, smelled, and smoked dope. Marijuana was the "sta-ple of hippiedom," declared *Time*, "L.S.D. its caviar," and [journalist] Nicholas von Hoffman added, "if the word means anything, it means a hippie is a dope dealer." At the end of the decade a journalist summed up the older generations' level of knowledge of the counterculture when he gave his peers ad-vice on how to spot a hippie: "Well, hippies look like hippies."

Americans like packages, labels. "Hippie" had been de-fined, so suburbanites turned away in disgust instead of trying to understand the rebellion. Actually, hippies considered themselves part of an alternative culture or underground, and they called each other many names, as a flyer proclaimed:

The Paisley Power Caucus of the Peace and Freedom Party

will hopefully prove congenial for hippies, Provos, anar-
chists, beatniks, Diggers, musicians, Zen monks, dealers,
utopians, Wobblies, calligraphers, felons, Boo Hoos, and the
many *UNCLASSIFIABLE* individuals who generally share
our perspective.

Usage of these terms changed over time and varied with
location. Some who felt part of the counterculture called
themselves "seekers" or because they used dope, "heads." During the second wave many used "hippie" or another popular
term, "freak," a "far out person" who was too odd, too abnor-
mal to be part of the normal society. . . .

No Requirements for Membership

Freaks cannot be discarded as simply "sex, drugs, and rock-
and-roll," because like the broader movement the counterculture included everyone, excluded no one. There were no hippie organizations, no membership cards, no meetings, no age
limits, no perquisites. Being a hippie often was an individual-
istic journey. One did not *have to* drop out for a semester, a
year, or a decade to "qualify" as a hippie, or *have to* take drugs,
participate in sex orgies, live in a commune, listen to rock,
grow long hair. No minimum requirements. No *have to*. While
some hippies might not be able to articulate their thoughts or
define their existence, most would agree that being part of the
counterculture was a frame of mind, like being part of the
movement [the protest element of the counterculture]. "Some
of the most longhaired people I know are bald," laughed [ac-
tivist] Jerry Rubin, and when a professor at the University of
Utah criticized the counterculture, a student responded: "The
hippie movement is not a beard, it is not a weird, colorful cos-
tume, it is not marijuana. The hippie movement . . . is a philosophy, a way of life, and a hippie is one who believes in this."
Some dropped out and became as apolitical as possible, others
participated in what they considered was a cultural revolution,
but most rejected the values of the predominant culture and
then developed and practiced different lifestyles. While this
seemed difficult for the older generation to comprehend, it
was readily understood by freaks all over the nation.

Moreover, hippies did not need older experts to explain

the counterculture—they wrote about it constantly. Careful observers and later historians would have realized that by the end of the decade, as one thoughtful scholar noted: "The lesson to be learned from the turbulent youthquake is not that long hair or body odor or disrespect for traditional values are undermining the stability of America. The lesson for America is that *something is terribly wrong* with the systems that create such youthful unrest. And who are the most outspoken critics of these systems? Pick up an underground newspaper in Ann Arbor, Michigan, Jackson, Mississippi, Middle Earth, Iowa, New York, Chicago, or Los Angeles.". . .

Reacting to a Troubled World

The older generation was fighting a war, one that many younger citizens felt was illegal, inhumane, and immoral. For draft-age youth, the war forced a response. A young man could either go along with the establishment and join the military, fight the machine by protesting and resisting the draft, or drop out. The first two had not stopped the war, and after Nixon's election it was clear that the conflict would continue for years. What to do? [Musician] Country Joe McDonald answered, "You take drugs, you turn up the music very loud, you dance around, you build yourself a fantasy world where everything's beautiful."

Most kids blamed the war on the older generation. "What's happening," wrote an activist, "is that a whole generation is starting to say to its parents, 'You can no longer get us to kill & be killed for your uptight archaic beliefs.'" Many returning soldiers agreed. Unlike fathers coming home after World War II, Vietnam veterans rarely talked of heroism, duty, honor. Instead, the "endless war" became an endless barrage of horror stories and disillusionment. "I just lost respect for everything after Vietnam," Lieut. Al Wilder commented. "Everything I learned as a kid turned out to be a damn lie." The agonizing onslaught of war tales and images repulsed more and more of the sixties generation. . . .

Other kids were distressed by a nation that continued to discriminate against some of its own citizens. One son asked his parents: "'What would you do if a Negro moved in next door?' and they'd say, 'Nothing! We don't mind. And I'd say,

'What would you do if I wanted to marry a Negro?' and that was completely different. 'No. You can't marry a Negro. No, no. You can't do that.' And I couldn't understand why, because I'd been raised to believe Negroes were just like anyone else. Two and two just never made four."

Young blacks and whites, of course, had been mingling throughout the decade. On civil rights marches and during Mississippi Freedom Summer many participants reported feelings of personal liberation mixed with community, and later interracial contacts increased on campuses, in liberal cities, and in Southeast Asia. "Vietnam aligned us with blacks after years of encountering them only through music," recalled Toby Thompson. "Our parents may have orchestrated Vietnam, but we played it, taking a curious dividend from that horror. We shook hands with black language, marijuana, G.I. hip. . . . The war to erase communism created a fresh sense of community." Naturally, there was some friction between hippies and "spades," as they first were called in Haight-Ashbury [the San Francisco haven for hippies]. The hippies had been ingrained with the values of the white suburbs and were attempting to lose those beliefs, while many blacks were working to escape poverty and to join the middle class. Nevertheless, black culture influenced many young whites, through not only jazz and soul music but Martin Luther King's emphasis on nonviolence and love, two important themes of the counterculture. . . .

Thus, the behavior of the culture boosted the counterculture. Without racism, war, and campus paternalism, the population of hippiedom would have been proportionately about the same size as that of the beats in the postwar society. There would have been more hippies, of course, because of the enormous number of baby boomers, but the counterculture would have been relatively small, confined to the usual bohemian enclaves of the East and West coasts and a few college towns. . . .

Hypocrisy Among the Older Generation

Yet the counterculture expanded. National problems persisted, ran amok during the Nixon era, and that confirmed the hippie idea that the country was becoming a wasteland. By the end of the decade, surveys found that most citizens agreed with the statement, "Something is wrong with America."

To many youth, the great American institutions seemed to be failing, and that contradicted their upbringing. The military of the "greatest power on earth," a country that had "never lost a war," could not beat peasants in a tiny nation in Southeast Asia. The "experts" had supported this war. So had the political "leaders" in Washington and many "intellectuals" in New York. "The Right War at the Right Time." Students quickly realized that the draft was unfair. Harvard student James Fallows lost enough weight so his 6'1" frame was below minimum requirements, 120 pounds, while unaware working-class kids passed the physical and were shipped out for 'Nam. After graduation, many students felt that the future held out a

The Illusion of Abundance

In San Francisco the hippie ethic of brotherhood and kindness prompted a local group called the Diggers to open a "free store" where donated items were distributed at no cost to those in need. However, as Alex Forman, a former worker at the free store, recounts, the hippies had a rather preconceived notion of what need really was.

For a while I worked with a group in the Haight called the Diggers, who had a kind of a primitive communism view that was just "share all the wealth." The Diggers set up a free store, and people could just come in and take whatever they needed, and we fed people for free in the park.

At one point I realized the absurdity of that when these people from the neighborhood, these older black women, came into the free store and said, "How much do these clothes cost in here?" We said, "Oh, it's all free. You just take what you need, and then if you have extra, you give." They said, "What do you mean, you just take what you need?" "Well, you just take what you need, that's all." They said, "Really?"

So they came back with these big boxes and they started just taking tons of stuff off the racks. We said, "What are job in a sterile corporation, perhaps one that made napalm or polluted the environment. And for solace, the younger generation could turn to their ministers—the older generation who preached love your neighbor in segregated churches and who flinched at the sight of young worshipers not dressed in their "Sunday best."

Furthermore, during the age of euphemism there seemed an overload of inconsistencies, ironies, and contradictions. The nation made a hero of rocket scientist Wernher Von Braun, a former Nazi and enemy, while putting young college graduates in jail for years because they resisted military service that would send them to kill Vietnamese. Young Americans were old

you doing?" They said, "Well, you said take what you need." We said, "Yeah, well, you don't need all those clothes for yourself." They said, "No, but we need the money, so we're going to take the clothes and sell them."

They were in real scarcity, you know, they needed money, and here we were saying just take what you need for your own personal, immediate needs. But for them, that wasn't reality. Their reality was, "How are we going to get some money, and here's these foolish white people just letting us take whatever we need. Well, we need it all. We don't have anything."

That was the illusion of the whole hippie ethos, that there was this abundance. I think the hippie movement started in California—and was most powerful here—because there is this illusion of abundance here. Fruits were falling from the trees, rent was cheap, there were places to stay, the weather was tolerable even in the winter, there was a community of people who were into sharing. But there wasn't an abundance. There was an abundance at a certain time for certain people.

Joan Morrison and Robert K. Morrison, *From Camelot to Kent State: The Sixties Experience in the Words of Those Who Lived It.* New York: Oxford University Press, 1987, pp. 220–21.

enough, 18, to fight a war that they did not create, but not old enough, 21 then, to drink a beer or vote for their commander-in-chief. Doctors wrote 150 million prescriptions a year for tranquilizers and amphetamines, and parents who consumed caffeine, alcohol, and nicotine condemned youth for "using drugs."

Hippies turned the tables. It was not the younger generation that "blew it," but the older who behaved abnormally, who had lost touch with reality. Kids wondered, who was sane? As they watched popular films on campuses asking that question—*King of Hearts, A Thousand Clowns*—the establishment provided them with food for thought. The U.S. Supreme Court ruled that language was not obscene as long as it had "redeeming social value." A senator introduced a bill to "outlaw the Mafia." The federal Bureau of Reclamation announced plans to build dams on the Colorado River and flood the Grand Canyon. The federal government subsidized growing tobacco and at the same time paid for advertisements proclaiming that cigarettes were harmful to health and told college students that if they smoked marijuana they would "graduate to heroin." While some officials complained that a stamp picturing Henry David Thoreau made the author look too much like a hippie, President Nixon awarded Elvis Presley with a citation for the singer's contribution in the fight against drugs. . . .

By the end of the sixties, then, the smiling baby boomers who had entered college at mid-decade and attended classes during the days of decision, had graduated into a sea of frustration. "We do not feel like a cool, swinging generation," declared a Radcliffe graduate, "we are eaten up inside by an intensity that we cannot name.". . .

The counterculture believed that the nation had become a Steppenwolf, a berserk monster, a cruel society that made war on peasants abroad and at home beat up on minorities, dissidents, students, and hippies. America the Beautiful was no more; it had been replaced by Amerika the Death Culture. It was no coincidence that many youth no longer stood at sporting events as bands played the national anthem, or that one of their favorite groups took the name the Grateful Dead, or that more kids were using drugs. "What is increasingly clear," wrote one participant, "is that drugs are not a dangerous shortcut to ecstasy so much as they are a device used for coping with modern society. Drugs are . . . a desperate, futile flailing at a society that increasingly rejects humanitarian values." Many agreed with [Harvard professor and LSD advocate] Timothy Leary: "Your only hope is dope."

"There must be some way out of here," sang Jimi Hendrix. Alienation drove students toward the counterculture, for a hippie creed was that institutions and experts had failed. . . .

Hypocrisy. There were double standards, for boys and girls, for children and parents, for individuals and government. The struggle had cracked the consensus, student power revealed the contradictions, and the war killed the moral authority of the elders. "It is not only that parents are no longer guides," wrote Margaret Mead, "but that there are no guides."

Young against Old, but it never was that simple, for a number of elders understood the reasons for the counterculture. Martin Luther King felt that hippies resulted from the tragic debasement of American life, the slaughter in Southeast Asia, "the negative effect of society's evils on sensitive young minds." A bookstore manager said of hippies: "I don't blame these people for looking at us and shaking their heads. I think we handed them a lot of tough problems and I'm not sure what I'd be doing if I was growing up right now." A truck driver added, "I get a big kick outa hearin' about 'em, the drugs and shacking up together and given' the big guys hell," and a woman added: "Let 'em go their own way. They're not killing anybody. Our government's the one that's doin' that!". . .

Complete Disillusionment

By the second wave the sixties generation was clubbed into reality: The older generation was not practicing what it preached. Nor were some of the younger generation—the activists who had become revolutionaries, who clamored that there was no democracy in America and then shouted down other speakers while yelling Power to the People. As one demonstrator lamented, "the radicals always regard the people . . . as something to be manipulated, exploited, or ignored. 'Get out of the way, people,' they say, 'so we can have our revolution!'. . . Power trips are what we are trying to get away from." It wasn't that the emerging counterculture disagreed with the radical interpretation of America, it was that by the Nixon era that message was irrelevant. Fewer and fewer attended SDS [Students for a Democratic Society, a radical activist group] meetings while more and more meandered to the smoke-in and lay in the grass. While the self-proclaimed vanguard was only a tiny percentage of the movement, it eventually provoked many to drop out. "Why did we start collectives?" asked members of the Canyon Collective. "Because we didn't dig being bossed around by bureaucrats whether on the job or in 'the movement.' We were tired of living and acting alone, and wanted to share more of our lives with each other.". . .

As disillusionment soared after the assassination of Robert Kennedy [in 1968], activist Marvin Garson wondered: "What's wrong with the New Left? What happened to all the magic in phrases like 'participatory democracy' and 'let the people decide'?" He answered his own question: "The heartbreaker has been that for some reason people don't WANT to go to meetings, don't WANT to participate."

The stark realization that working in mainstream society would not change *the* world stimulated many activists to begin looking inside to change *their* world. As Ten Years After sang:

I'd love to change the world,
but I don't know what to do,
so I'll leave it up to you.

During the second wave changing their world usually was done two different ways—some left the cities and began building their own communes and alternative societies, and others stayed in hip communities usually near campuses and became cultural activists.

Universities became filled with people who looked, acted, and talked like hippies. After the Columbia University upheaval, Carl Davidson of SDS suggested that three-fourths of the organization's national membership could be classified as hippies, and at Rutgers and Long Island universities professors noted interest waning from politics. "Now the talk has shifted to cultural revolution. Gentle grass is pushing up through the cement." Students who had been involved in protests began to look inward, and even occupying a campus building became part of a personal revolution. "The idea was to liberate yourself from the confining conventions of life, and to celebrate the irrational side of your nature, kind of let yourself go," recalled a University of Chicago student. "This was the counterculture coming to us, and it stirred people up and made us feel like doing something dramatic."

To many, doing something dramatic meant doing something *different*, rejecting the values drilled into them as they grew up during cold war culture. "The point is that it was the culture that was sick," said Jentri Anders. "One way to change that is to live it differently . . . just drop out and live it the way you think it ought to be."

What It Meant to Drop Out

Live differently, outside of the mainstream, but of course freaks never could drop out completely. They drove the roads and had to adhere to highway laws, bought land and had to comply with local ordinances. They paid rent, bills, and had to buy food and other goods. Some worked and paid taxes, others used social services, and some got drafted.

Dropping out, then, usually meant dropping the values of the older generation—developing ones for the New America—and counterculture values were a reaction to mainstream ones. . . .

When straights [non-hippies] talked about "traditional values," freaks became the movement's cultural shock troops. During the first wave almost all activists had short hair and appeared and behaved rather clean-cut, but hippies delighted in upsetting the older generation with their dress, language, and especially hair. "I never could tell where my husband's sideburns ended and his mustache began," recalled a baby boomer, "but he didn't care as long as it irritated his mother.". . .

Instead of the straight, normal life, [guitarist with the folk-rock band Country Joe and the Fish] Barry Melton recalled, "We were setting up a new world . . . that was going to run parallel to the old world but have as little to do with it as possible. We just weren't going to deal with straight people."

Become a freak. Adopt different values. If the average guy took the straight and narrow road, the superhighway to suburbs, hippies sought another path, dancing to a different drummer. . . .

Many became seekers, dropping out for a while, searching for themselves and for America. New spaces. New experiences. New thoughts. . . .

Pleasure Seeking

Many did, as the second wave became the "Age of Aquarius," a joyous, bright time, a new morning. "Here comes the sun," proclaimed the Beatles, and the musicians in *Hair* sang out, "Let the sun shine." "The hippies have passed beyond American society," wrote an underground journalist. "They're not really living in the same society. It's not so much that they're living on the leftovers, on the waste of American society, as that they just don't give a damn."

They did give a damn about their own culture, however, and they began to build one that expressed values that they felt were positive, healthy—building a peaceful, gentle society that discriminated against no one and that practiced love. . . .

A theme of cold war culture (and a later era) was "just say no." The creed was the Protestant Ethic: work. The motif of the sixties was "just say yes," and the canon was the Pleasure Ethic: fun. Live for the moment. Have a Happy Day.

Freaks said yes to many things that their parents had told them to reject—especially drugs and sex. . . .

Dope was the freak's little helper that aided their escape from the establishment. . . . Escape was important. Frustrated people often relieve anxieties by eating, smoking, drinking, even shopping away their worries: "I Love to Shop!" But not hippies. "Smoke dope everywhere," proclaimed one. "Dope is Great, it's fun, it's healthy. . . . Get every creature so stoned they can't stand the plastic shit of American culture.". . .

Thus, by taking dope hippies felt different, Heads [short for Dope Heads] versus Straights, another form of Us versus Them. "Grass opened up a new space for middle class white kids," recalled Jay Stevens, "an inner space as well as outer space. It became a ritual—sitting around with your friends, passing a joint from person to person, listening to music, eating, talking, joking, maybe making out—all the senses heightened." They felt community being part of the underground. . . .

A majority of the sixties generation, then, tried marijuana, and many more attempted to liberate themselves from the older generation's sexual mores. Elders had taught children Puritan values, that sex was reserved for married adults. Youth must avoid premarital sex and promiscuity, and rumors abounded that masturbation caused everything from blindness to hand warts.

The sledgehammer to prevent such behavior was GUILT. Hippies rebelled, calling those ideas "hang-ups" and advocating "free love." Of course, they did not invent the idea, for armed with birth control pills the sixties generation had been experimenting at college and sexual freedom leagues had been established earlier in the Bay Area and New York City. But freaks expanded the idea so sex seemed freer than at any time in memory. "Let's spend the night together" wailed the Rolling Stones, while Janis Joplin advised her sisters to "get it while you can.". . .

Making love and smoking dope was behavior usually conducted behind closed doors; dress was for the public, and it was a symbol. Hair represented rebellion from the crew-cut cold war era, and identity with the new generation. "Almost cut my hair," sang Crosby, Stills, and Nash, but instead they let their "freak flag fly," because, as Nash later stated, "if they had long hair you knew how they thought, that they were into good music, a reasonable life, that they probably hated the government." Hair, and dress, sequestered them from mom and pop, declared independence. Hip men threw out sport coats and ties, and hip women abandoned cosmetics and undergarments and for the first time in memory revealed the soft contours of unbound bodies. "Long hair, beards, no bras and freaky clothes represent a break from Prison Amerika," declared Jerry Rubin. Clothes became costumes and costumes became clothes.

The older generation was appalled, complaining, "you can't tell the boys from the girls," and oh, those "dirty, filthy, smelly hippies." During the veteran's era after World War II and Korea, the sight of a beard on a businessman even raised eyebrows. But freaks had different ideas about dress and cleanliness. While they did bathe, of course, they were not dismayed by the smell of the human body, for it was normal, part of getting back to nature and a revolt against middle-class TV-commercial values. They felt that deodorant, cosmetics, perfume, cologne were phony, Madison Avenue: "Aren't you glad you use Dial? Don't you wish everybody did?" Don't care, said the freaks, saying that people should smell their bodies, for each individual's scent was different. Learn about yourself: "You're beautiful." If they desired a scent then they lit incense or wore musk oil, a secretion of the male musk deer. Hippies also abandoned polyester clothing in favor of leather and cotton, and they ate fresh, natural foods without preservatives and grown organically.

Not "uptight," but "laid back" in dress and also in lifestyle. Many critics labeled hippies "lazy," and parents claimed, "You're throwing your life away. You don't know how hard it was for us. . . ." But that missed the point about hip ideas of work and play. "Life should be ecstasy," said Allen Ginsberg, and hippies worked to escape daily drudgery and to discover their own pleasureful existence. . . .

Finding a Home

Hippiedom was gentle for some, groping on a sunny afternoon, throwing frisbees with friends, and for others it was a continual excursion as they donned backpacks, put out their thumbs, and caught the disease—wanderlust. "If the vibes are good, I'll stay on," [a hippie named] Joanie said about New Jerusalem commune, "if not, I've heard about a Zen group in the Sierras I'd like to look into." The quest did not end at U.S. borders. The demand for passports doubled, and by the end of the decade about 800,000 young Americans were traveling in Europe while over a million were thumbing throughout the nation. "We weren't fleeing home," said one, "we were seeking one."

Folk Music Fosters a New Political Awareness

Richie Unterberger

The resurgence of interest in folk music accompanied the cultural shift that took place in America during the 1960s. Although some of the folk music of the decade was copied from or inspired by older songs and styles, new artists imbued it with a fresh vitality and a more contemporary message that matched the turbulence of the times.

Greenwich Village in the heart of New York City was the epicenter of the 1960s folk movement. It was here, in clubs like Gerde's Folk City, the Cafe Wha?, the Gaslight, and in public spaces like Washington Square Park, that young people witnessed and participated in the folk-music revival. Although interest in folk music was spreading elsewhere in the country, the Village was awash in young and old talent, and many initiates made a pilgrimage there to enrich their understanding of folk traditions.

As the New York scene began to grow, opportunists recognized the potential to cash in on the wealth of talent flourishing there. By creating management institutions and publishing companies, entrepreneurs helped to nurture and exploit the future stars of a generation. Once these edifices were in place, the folk scene in New York was set to expand into a broader market. In addition, a nationwide audience was ready to go beyond the revelry encour-

■

aged by rock-and-roll music and discover a new music that delivered a mature, meaningful message.

In the following article, music historian and critic
Richie Unterberger explains how many artists who
worked in the folk tradition started out by learning
songs that were written before most of the artists
were even born; and, aside from slight interpretive
variation, the songs differed little from the age-old
originals. When Bob Dylan began to make waves in
the folk community by developing his own compositions in 1962, Unterberger notes that other artists responded in kind, producing a swell of new music that
dealt with political issues of the day. Songs that spoke
out against everything from the war in Vietnam to
the dangers of capitalism at home proliferated
through the culture, raising the awareness of an already awakening generation. Soon, record sales and
chart positions of folk artists like Peter, Paul & Mary
reflected a growing acceptance of folk music into the
mainstream. As Unterberger attests, by the middle of
the sixties, folk music had arrived at the forefront of
America's attention as both a commercial force and a
catalyst for social change.

Richie Unterberger is a senior editor for the *All
Music Guide*. He has written several books on rock-
and-roll music, including *Unknown Legends of Rock 'n'
Roll*, the *Rough Guide to Music USA*, and *Turn! Turn!
Turn!: The '60s Folk-Rock Revolution*, from which this
excerpt is taken.

WHERE DYLAN MADE HIS MOST RADICAL BREAK
from previous generations [of folk performers] was not so
much through his style as through his songwriting. . . .

Over the course of 1962 his writing matured both lyrically
and melodically. His second album, *The Freewheelin' Bob Dylan*
(released in May 1963), was comprised almost wholly of original material, . . . a bold step for a folksinger who had yet to secure a national reputation.

The very issue of whether artists identifying themselves as

"folk" musicians should be writing songs at all had been an issue of some controversy in the folk community since the onset of the folk revival (and continues to engender less heated debate even now). If pressed for a definition of what constituted a "folk" song, many would have classified it as a song of no known certain author or origin, having been shaped by collective forces and passed down through the generations. . . .

[Folk pioneers Pete] Seeger, [Woody] Guthrie, and others may have written effective songs of social commentary and personal experience, albeit often based on old folk melodies (as, indeed, many of Dylan's early tunes were). There were substantial numbers of absolutists, though, who viewed folk that had been shaped by the folk process as its only true manifestation. Songwriters could be dismissed as being outside of the music's realm, or even desecrators of the tradition.

On *The Freewheelin' Bob Dylan* and his third album (*The Times They Are A-Changin'*, released at the beginning of 1964), Dylan nudged folk closer to the mainstream of popular culture—and hence, though no one could have foreseen it, rock music—by writing both personal songs that tapped into his generation's zeitgeist, and observational ones that directly or allegorically commented upon social issues. "Blowin' in the Wind," its pensive angst reflecting an uncertain world that had tottered to the edge of self-immolation, was the most famous. . . .

[Member of the band the Holy Modal Rounders, Pete] Stampfel: "No one really thought much about writing songs until Dylan came along, although Tom Paxton was writing songs, and of course Pete Seeger was also. But it was very uncommon. It seems that a lot of people, watching Dylan make up songs, suddenly felt that *they* had to do it, or felt that it was alright to do it, or that [it] was expected of them. Whereas people didn't have that feeling when hearing Tom Paxton songs, which preceded Dylan's by a couple of years. When I started writing songs, I mostly did it the way Dylan started writing songs in 1961, which is putting new words to old songs, which of course is what Woody Guthrie did a lot before Dylan. . . .

"We all thought that Bob was phenomenal," says Tom Paxton. "Songwriters love to hear good songs, and it really had the effect of spurring us to keep trying to improve our writing. It just happened that a lot of the good songs we heard were from

Bob. . . . They made me want to write great songs myself."

[Folk artist] Buffy Sainte-Marie looks back on the genesis of a new songwriting consciousness with affection, and sees how the folk revival spawned a new audience and performance environment that made such compositions possible: "Our early-'60s generation had the great benefit of a network of coffeehouses which attracted students. My songs—because of that special window of student-powered coffeehouse communication—could be about anything, and still have an audience. Early-'60s songs were real, beyond the old Sinatra/Eisenhower Tin Pan Alley themes. As a songwriter I had the benefit of hearing real folk songs, and tried to write songs that would last for generations (like an antique) and be universal in appeal. That is, (typical college girl approach) I did real research and had no familiarity with the business part of the music business, so I wasn't 'aiming at a market.' The songs were original, unusual, well-researched, and most of all true to what I was seeing around me, which rang true to student audiences and other artists across a wide range of styles."

The Folk Scene Gets Some Help

Broadside magazine was an important agent in fostering a new, socially conscious generation of writers—"topical" songwriters, as they were called at the time. Its impact was felt not so much through the magazine itself, which began as a mimeographed seven-page job with a print run of a mere 300 in February 1962 (by the mid-'60s, circulation was still only a thousand, and even at its peak would not exceed 2,500). Its contribution was providing a forum for new songwriters who usually had yet to land big record deals, or record at all. The issues were centered around printed lyrics and rudimentary sheet music to new compositions, aiming to—as issue #2 declared—"distribute topical songs and stimulate the writing of such songs. Our policy is to let each songwriter speak freely—even though we may not agree fully with the sentiments expressed—and let each song cut its own trail.". . .

Sometimes the magazine would even make its own primitive recordings in Folkways' studio, or on a cheap reel-to-reel recorder in the apartment of *Broadside* editors Sis Cunningham (herself a musician) and Gordon Friesen, some of which found release through the Folkways label (including some cuts by Bob Dylan under the pseudonym Blind Boy Grunt). The editorial content expanded to include interviews and provocative essays, such as one on "The Need for Topical Music" by Phil Ochs, who would contribute several lengthy pieces to *Broadside* over the coming years. "I think there is a coming revolution in folk music as it becomes more and more popular in the US, and as the search for new songs becomes more intense," wrote Ochs. "The news today is the natural resource that folk music must exploit in order to have the most vigorous folk process possible.". . .

Bob Dylan's inventive and passionate lyrics became an anthem for a generation and marked a pivotal turning point in folk music.

Many of the songs they recorded for Broadside/Folkways releases, and/or printed in the pages of *Broadside*, in the early and mid-'60s can be heard on the Smithsonian Folkways five-CD box set *The Best of Broadside, 1962–1988.* The execution and melodies can be plain and dry, the lyrics more blunt than poetic. But even at their most ham-handed, they were targeting maladies of the contemporary world, and not just promoting remnants of Depression-era American radicalism. There were songs about fears of nuclear war, critiques of US imperialism, cries for justice for African-Americans, and rage at media manipulation. . . .

In such a fashion, the influence of *Broadside*—and, by extension, the Communist- and socialist-rooted progressive politics of Americans like Cunningham and Freisen—spread far beyond its tiny circulation base.

"They helped to foster that sense of community," says [folksinger Janis] Ian. "Otherwise it just would've been a bunch of people running around the Village trying to make it. Sis and Gordon had something more noble in mind. They really mentored two generations of songwriters. If you look at the amount of people who were published there for the first time, from Dylan and Phil Ochs to me, it's extraordinary how people gravitated to them. They were there when you were in trouble, they were there when you were celebrating, they were there to listen to anything new that you wrote and offer their opinions, they were there if you needed to sleep on their couch. You don't find that anymore. . . ."

"It was a place where we could write songs, have them actually appear in print, and learn from each other," adds Paxton. "And be part of something that was bigger than ourselves. In the context of those years, the civil rights movement and then the war in Vietnam, it was very important to us to have a place where songs on those and related topics could appear. Songs that had, really, very little or no commercial possibilities, nevertheless were appearing in print."

Commercial Success

Yet some of those songs *did* have commercial possibilities, as did some of those performers. The signing of topical songwriters to proper record labels (Broadside, and its distributor Folkways, didn't have the muscle to sell many units) really didn't get underway in a big way until 1964. But when it did, many of the better singer-songwriters whose early work can be heard on the *Broadside* box were recording for the biggest independent folk labels, and sometimes even major ones like Columbia. . . .

At that point, it would have been difficult for many of the topical songwriters to sell great quantities of their own records. . . . Song publishing, in addition to record sales, is where much of the real earning potential lies in the music industry. Labels, managers, and publishers knew that some of the new breed's songs could be far bigger if they were given the right interpretation. . . .

One of those visionaries on the lookout for songs to publish and record was Albert Grossman. He had engineered the formation, after considering various possible members . . . of the two-man-plus-one-woman vocal folk trio Peter, Paul & Mary. Their work has not worn well with rock-oriented critics, who scorn the tame, clean-cut precision of their arrangements; their broad cross-generational appeal; . . . and their dilution of songs that were recorded in more cutting, emotional versions by their composers.

There is no denying, however, the enormous impact of Peter, Paul & Mary's self-titled 1962 debut album, which went to #1 and stayed on the chart for two years. And there were real reasons for their popularity that went beyond clever managerial strategy. Their harmonies were ebullient, with a far greater sense of rhythmic joie de vivre than the standard pop-folk act. Their personas interacted dynamically, with the sex appeal of Mary Travers, the comic interjections of Noel "Paul" Stookey, and the more serious musicianship of Peter Yarrow. Their choice of material, often under the guidance of Grossman, was astute. And if they weren't the most down-home port of entry, they nonetheless did their share to turn many on to the riches of traditional folk music. "Peter, Paul & Mary brought a lot of fairly esoteric folk music to the public attention by playing a quite bland version of it, that then could direct you toward something a little stiffer," believes John Sebastian [of the Lovin' Spoonful]. . . .

The Top Ten hit off their first LP was Pete Seeger and Lee Hays's "If I Had a Hammer" (first recorded as a single by the

Weavers in 1949), a rallying cry for brotherhood, sisterhood, justice, and freedom. To get a folk song into the Top Ten was difficult enough in 1962. To do so with a song that had first been performed at a benefit for Communist Party leaders that had been prosecuted under the Smith Act[1] was nothing short of astounding, though no doubt many if not most of those buying Peter, Paul & Mary singles were unaware of its origins and socialist, pro-labor overtones.

The group seemed to be taking a greater risk by putting out a single of Dylan's "Blowin' in the Wind," which they first heard as an acetate passed on to them by Grossman, and which had already been released by the New World Singers (on a *Broadside* compilation) and the Chad Mitchell Trio before they put it on a 45 in June 1963. Dylan was, after all, at this point still a far less famous and acclaimed songwriter than Seeger. Yet the single made #2, greatly advancing not just the career of both Peter, Paul & Mary and Dylan, but also the overall crossover of folk to the pop audience. Another Dylan cover by Peter, Paul & Mary, "Don't Think Twice, It's All Right," followed "Blowin' in the Wind" into the Top Ten later in 1963. In helping expose the trio to fellow client Dylan, Grossman was, in Yarrow's estimation, "giving a gift of a possibility of discovering extraordinarily written material to us. We were *all* a family."

It might be tempting to accuse the musicians and their manager of financial self-interest in their raids of the Dylan catalog. Since he handled both Dylan and PP&M (as they were often abbreviated), and took fully 50% of Dylan's publishing income, Grossman had much to gain by getting Dylan's songs to be hits. Hit covers made Dylan more famous and brought substantial publishing revenue for both Grossman and Dylan. Peter, Paul & Mary were hardly unwitting pawns in Grossman's game, however. Not only was their enthusiasm for Dylan's music genuine, but so was their commitment to the progressive humanism espoused by "Blowin' in the Wind" and "If I Had a Hammer." It was backed up by appearances at events such as the summer 1963 March on Washington for civil rights, at which Dylan also played.

---

1. The Smith Act was a 1940 law that made it illegal to advocate the violent overthrow of the government. It was aimed at the Communist Party in the United States.

Peter, Paul & Mary's recordings of Dylan material were indicative of a new eagerness throughout contemporary folk in general to broaden repertoire from a traditional base and encompass new, emerging songwriters. . . .

On Judy Collins's third album, #3 (from late 1963), she took the then-daring step of devoting most of the set to contemporary material. There were a couple of Dylan tunes, but also work by Hamilton Camp, Bob Gibson, Shel Silverstein (an accomplished folk songwriter, though he's better known as a *Playboy* cartoonist and composer of Dr. Hook's "The Cover of Rolling Stone") Mike Settle, and Pete Seeger. . . .

"I had made two albums which were basically traditional," says Collins. "We sat down and said, wait a minute. There's a whole raft of these wonderful writers—the city singers, the city writers, the music coming out of the contemporary folk scene. I was aware of, and surrounded by, these great writers, including of course Dylan. I saw Pete Seeger all the time, heard him, went to his concerts. . . . So I was very attuned to the music, and I loved it. I think that my third album was an important album in the folk process, because I think it did bring people's attention to a lot of these songs that were being written by the singer-songwriters of the time.". . .

Folk Reaches Greater Acceptance

By late 1963, folk music was at its greatest level of acceptance and popularity within the pop world. Peter, Paul & Mary and Joan Baez were selling more LPs than almost anyone. PP&M had made Top Ten singles, and other acts were taking occasional songs into the top of the chart, as did the Rooftop Singers (with Erik Darling, who had been in a later Weavers lineup) with their #1 "Walk Right In," an adaptation of a song first issued in 1930 by the Memphis jug-blues band Cannon's Jug Stompers. Trini Lopez somehow managed to get to #3 with another version of "If I Had a Hammer," only a year after Peter, Paul & Mary. The New Christy Minstrels made the Top 20 with "Green, Green," featuring the hoarse lead vocals of Barry McGuire. . . .

On top of its commercial presence, folk was more in tune with the mood of the American audience than it had ever been. The crumbling of the worst aspects of McCarthyism and the

Cold War had led the way for new freedom of expression. There was overdue advocacy for civil rights for African-Americans, a cause with which many folk musicians, white and black, allied themselves. College-age political activists were making their own break with outmoded tradition by building a New Left in the Students for a Democratic Society. President John F. Kennedy, for all his considerable flaws, kindled hope for progressive social change and decreased discrimination with the more liberal aspects of his agenda, as well as projecting youthful energy that many young liberals felt mirrored their own. "Why are we in the midst of a folk boom?" asked Dylan in the *New York Sunday News* that October. "Because the times cry for the truth and that's what they're hearin' in good folk music today."

"Do you realize the power of folk music?" queried Peter Yarrow in a *Saturday Evening Post* cover story on the folk boom. "Do you realize the power of PP&M? We could mobilize the youth of America today in a way that no one else could. We could conceivably travel with a presidential candidate, and maybe even sway an election. Not that we're going to use this power. It's enough to know that we have it. . . . I'm part of a group and a movement that is saying to people, 'We care about you, we want you to feel our love, we're not trying to feed you placebo tablets'. . . . We're not out to protest anything. Our purpose is to affirm. We get up on stage to show how beautiful it is to open your heart, to feel pity, to cry, to get involved."

"Folk music had become the dominant music on the airwaves in America around 1963," says Yarrow now. "What it brought to the scene was the full legacy of folk music as an expression of social consciousness, a way to create community, and really be a part of social change. When I say part of social change, I don't mean just as the trimming, but a kind of exchange of hearts connection that really energized and reflected the feelings of people, and ultimately their determination to forge a fairer and more just society. This music was filled with a sense of honesty that was untainted by the simple desire to make money, which was not necessarily the prevalent motivation for writing and singing music prior to the folk renaissance in the 1960s."

The times seemed ripe for folk music to act as an important vehicle for changing society.

The Accessible Motown Sound

Brian Ward

In 1959 Berry Gordy, an ambitious black entrepreneur and record label manager, formed Motown Records in Detroit, Michigan. Motown was just one of many related labels that Gordy operated in addition to a publishing company and talent agency. Hitsville USA, as Motown was dubbed, drew in various artists who were willing to be shaped by Gordy's overriding mantra that his records would avoid blues clichés and be palatable to audiences outside the black community. Several performers such as Smokey Robinson, Marvin Gaye, and Mary Wells joined the Motown family and cut hit records under Gordy's paternal guidance. Critics bashed the resulting "Motown sound" as too calculated and far too acquiescent to white radio, but listeners of all colors embraced the pop beat of the music and the glitzy image of the Motown artists.

In the following selection, Brian Ward discusses the creation of the Motown sound, its fans, and its detractors. According to Ward, Motown may have had a signature sound, but its music was also quite diverse. In his opinion, critics who portray Motown records as musically compromised tend to forget that many other black musical acts of the day were equally orchestrated. Furthermore, although critics tend to view Berry Gordy as too eager to sell his music to white audiences, Ward argues that all black artists in the 1960s were striving for commercial success and

■

Brian Ward, *Just My Soul Responding: Rhythm and Blues, Black Consciousness, and Race Relations*. Berkeley: University of California Press, 1998. Copyright © 1998 by The Regents of the University of California. Reproduced by permission.

wide appeal. Black audiences, moreover, did not seem to share the views of the critics. As Ward notes, they along with legions of other American fans bought into the Motown sound because of its musical appeal and danceable beat.

Brian Ward is a professor of history at the University of Newcastle upon Tyne in England. He teaches and writes on American history and has published three books including *Media, Culture, and the Modern African American Freedom Struggle* and *Just My Soul Responding: Rhythm and Blues, Black Consciousness, and Race Relations*, from which this article is taken.

CONSUMMATE MUSICIANS LIKE JAMES JAMERSON, Earl Van Dyke, Benny Benjamin (drums) and James Messina (guitar) were crucial in the development of what has become instantly recognizable, if analytically elusive, as the "Motown sound". Yet, given the oceans of print devoted to this "sound", one of the most striking features of Motown's early output was not its homogeneity, but its diversity.

Bluesy performers like Mabel Johns, Barrett Strong and Marv Johnson were initially balanced by coy girl groups like the Marvelettes and soloists like Mary Wells. Long-forgotten white acts like the Valadiers co-existed with the Four Tops, who at first found themselves on Gordy's Jazz Workshop subsidiary [record label] where they experimented with big band arrangements of Tin Pan Alley standards. The Supremes recorded everything from Rodgers and Hart tunes to country and western, and from a Sam Cooke tribute album to a collection of Beatles songs, hoping to find a winning formula. Meanwhile Marvin Gaye was encouraged to indulge his considerable talent for crooning on albums like *Hello Broadway* and *A Tribute to the Great Nat King Cole*. With such an eclectic mixture of styles, and Gordy's keen eye for any potentially lucrative market niche, it was easy to credit the 1962 *Detroit Free Press* article which announced that Motown was about to launch a line of polka records.

Eventually, however, Motown did more than just produce a diverse range of records, any one of which might appeal predominantly to a different market. It forged a flexible house style which appealed across regional, racial and even generational boundaries. "We were a general-market company. Whether you were black, white, green or blue, you could relate our music", Gordy rightly boasted. From the maelstrom of early experimentation, it was Martha Reeves who blazed the gospel-paved, string-lined trail to the label's mid-1960s crossover triumph. In the summer of 1963, [the songwriting team of] Holland-Dozier-Holland furnished Reeves with "Heatwave" and then "Quicksand" on which they enlivened the slightly mannered basics of the girl group sound with a driving gospel beat, tambourine frenzy and soaring strings. Above it all, Reeves, who was comfortably the finest female vocalist on Motown's books until Gladys Knight joined and ran her close in the 1960s, unleashed her rapt soul vocals.

The Magic Formula

Following the Top Ten pop success of these recordings, this basic formula was refined and adapted to fit the peculiar talents of individual Motown acts. The leonine roar of lead singer Levi Stubbs meant that the Four Tops retained the melodrama of the Vandellas' recordings on songs like "Reach out, I'll be there" and "Bernadette". By contrast, the Temptations harked back to their doowopping origins as the Primes to feature rich harmonies and a generally sweeter sound on Smokey Robinson–penned and produced songs like "It's growing" and "My girl". The most successful of all the Motown acts to work within this basic framework was the Supremes, for whom Holland-Dozier-Holland softened the hard-driving gospel beat with more prominent strings and muted brass. The mix was topped with vocals by Diana Ross which were much lighter and breathier than Martha's on chart-topping songs like "Where did our love go?" and "Baby love". The Supremes proved to be the perfect black crossover act. Between 1964 and Ross' departure from the group in 1969, they secured 25 pop hits, including 12 number ones—only the Beatles could claim more.

If there was a classic "Motown sound", neither its ubiquity nor its rigidity should be exaggerated; not even for the period between 1964 and 1967 when it was at its zenith. In 1965, Motown released the Miracles' soulful post-doowop lament "Ooo baby baby", Jr Walker's saxophone-led blues stomp "Shotgun", Stevie Wonder's grinding rock'n'soul remake of Tommy Tucker's "Hi heel sneakers", and Marvin Gaye's gospel shout, "Ain't that peculiar". All were highly successful, yet all somehow circumvented, or greatly extended, the basic formula.

Even those artists who stuck tight as a Benny Benjamin backbeat to the classic Motown sound, could, just like that precocious skinsman, actually produce a broad range of moods and shadings within its confines. Thus, 1965 also saw the release of the Temptations' melancholic "Since I lost my baby," the Contours' barnstorming "Can you jerk like me", the Four Tops' distraught "Ask the lonely", and the Vandellas' disturbing, claustrophobic masterpiece "Nowhere to run".

Despite this constrained diversity, however, the idea of a single Motown Sound, clinically designed by a team of songwriters, and producers led by Gordy, Robinson, Holland-Dozier-Holland, William Stevenson and Ivy Hunter, and mechanically riveted onto the label's recordings by musical artisans, pervades the literature. Not only is this view inaccurate, but it betrays an insidious form of racial stereotyping, and has become, in Jon Fitzgerald's phrase a "major impediment to general acknowledgement of Motown's role as a major *innovative* force in 1960s popular music".

Integrity in Question

The signs adorning the offices of Motown and Stax respectively—"Hitsville, USA" and "Soulsville, USA"—have frequently been taken to symbolize a completely different musical ethos, a different commercial agenda, and even a different degree of artistic and racial integrity between the two labels. Critics have regularly made unfavourable comparisons between the slick Motown soul production line and the more relaxed, spontaneous, atmosphere of southern labels like Stax, with their rootsier feel and country-fried licks. Paradoxically, southern soul, largely recorded on white-owned labels by integrated groups of musicians who drew on black and white musical influences, has been reified as more authentically black than the secularized gospel recordings of black musicians on a black-owned label with virtually no white creative input—at least not until English woman Pam Sawyer made a name for herself as a staff writer in the late 1960s with songs like the Supremes' "Love child".

Even the usually sensible [music critic] Arnold Shaw fell headlong into this trap, describing Motown in terms which made it sound like a pale imitation of something blacker, something more real, more substantial, lurking in the southlands. Motown songs, Shaw claimed, "are light and fluffy. It is hardly soul food, but rather a dish for which white listeners have acquired a taste". In a similar vein, Mike Jahn derided Motown as "a black-owned version of popular schmaltz", thereby recycling conventional stereotypes about the nature of "real" black music, much as Tony Cummings did when he casually dismissed Marvin Gaye's crooning as "appalling . . . ill-conceived mushmallow". Cummings was apparently unable to countenance even the possibility that a black American singer could be a magnificent interpreter of Tin Pan Alley Americana.

Critics have tended to privilege the recordings of Stax, Fame and their southern brethren over those of Motown, largely because the musicians who played on those southern sessions have been viewed as genuine artists, not artisans. Southern players, so the legend goes, improvised amazing riffs and spontaneously wove together sublime rhythmic and harmonic patterns from the very warp and weft of their souls. Those protean moments were then instantly committed to tape and transferred, unsullied, onto vinyl.

Contrary to this popular myth, however, southern soul records—with some exceptions—were rarely produced in single, improvised live takes. Overdubbing was common—even at Stax, where Otis Redding's oft-quoted statement that "we cut everything together, horns, rhythms and vocals . . . we didn't even have a four-track tape recorder. You can't over dub on a one-track machine" has been accepted as chapter and verse for all 1960s southern soul. In fact, even at Stax, vocals were frequently added after the instrumental tracks were laid down, and many records were assembled from carefully splicing together the best moments from alternate takes.

This is not to deny that southern studios had marvellously talented musicians whose long hours of practice and laid-back jamming generated moments of great musical invention and almost uncanny understanding. Rather it is to suggest that, just like at Motown, arrangers, producers and engineers were also vital in shaping the recorded, or more accurately, the released sound of southern soul records. . . .

Part of the problem in all of this has been a confusion between what it takes to be a great, creative, innovative musician, and what it takes to make great records. Of course, the two are not mutually exclusive, but they are certainly not synonymous. Rock and pop are full of wonderful records made by players of sorely limited musical ability who have barely known which end of a piano to blow, but who have been blessed with a fine ear for the combinations of words, rhythms and sounds which can move minds, bodies and souls. Even in Rhythm and Blues, where the calibre of musicians was generally high, neither technical proficiency nor simple sincerity were necessarily enough to guarantee a great record.

Given, then, that there was considerably more to making southern soul records than simply opening the mikes to pick up the sounds of innate black and/or white musical genius, the differences between the Stax and the Motown studios were rather less marked than the similarities. Motown's Funk Brothers mostly comprised gifted southern jazz exiles. Much like its integrated southern counterparts, it was a tight unit consisting of musicians who were simultaneously skilled craftsmen and trusty production workers, with a maverick streak of inventive genius bubbling to the surface every once in a glorious while. "They'd let me go on and ad-lib", explained James Jamerson, using precisely the term Jerry Wexler applied to the atmosphere in southern studios ("extremely ad lib"). "I created man", Jamerson insisted; "it was repetitious, but had to be funky and have emotion".

Bidding for the Mainstream

While there is no evidence that any black-oriented label or Rhythm and Blues artist ever sought anything less than the widest possible commercial success, it is nonetheless true that Berry Gordy went to extraordinary, often hugely creative, lengths to give his performers the opportunity to make it with white audiences. This was a matter of presentation as well as sound. Motown acts were formally schooled by Maxine Powell, the owner of a Detroit finishing and modelling school, in matters of etiquette, deportment, cosmetics and elocution. Gordy felt this might make them more acceptable to white America and an expanding black middle class for whom mainstream notions of respectability remained important.

Veteran dancer Cholly Atkins was hired to supervise the sophisticated stagecraft and slick choreography which was designed to equip Motown acts for the "transition from the chitlin' circuit to Vegas". Touring London in the autumn of 1964, Mary Wilson made no secret of Gordy's and the Supremes' crossover ambitions, and their willingness to adjust to white expectations to achieve them. "We want to get into the night-club field and we know we're going to have to change our style a good bit to get there. We're working on that kind of singing now . . . I know there's a lot of work ahead of us but we really hope to play the Copa some day". The following July, the Supremes became the first of many Motown acts to play that New York shrine of middle American wealth and respectability; in 1967 they were the first Motown artists to play the even ritzier Las Vegas Copa.

Music critics, far more than fans, have frequently struggled with the idea that showmanship, artifice and spectacle can sometimes be the vehicles, as well as adornments—or, worse, replacements—for genuine creativity, expression and artistic endeavour. Certainly, most accounts which focus on Motown's unapologetic pursuit of the mainstream market assume that it was simply impossible to produce a music which was artistically potent, truly expressive of aspects of contemporary mass black consciousness, and at the same time an ambitious showbiz phenomenon hugely popular with a biracial audience. For example, in a particularly pompous and insensitive 1967 article, rock critic Ralph Gleason used the fact that the Supremes and Four Tops were choreographed to support his claim that black soul performers were "almost totally style with very little substance". Gleason denounced them for being "on an Ed Sullivan trip, striving as hard as they can to get on that stage and become part of the American success story". In fact, as [music critic and sociologist] Simon Frith has recognized, "if some of Motown's marketing strategies have touched depths of cynicism that just makes its continued musical inspiration even more humbling".

The Black Fan Base

Motown's unparalleled popularity among black consumers suggests that the black masses shared little of the critics' sense of fakery and fraud. The corporation enjoyed 174 black Top Ten entries during the 1960s. Apparently unable to recognize "real" black music without the guidance of critics like Gleason, blacks even bought huge numbers of records by the Supremes, the bewigged flagship of Gordy's race treachery and integrationist aspirations, giving them 23 black hits and 5 number ones between the restoration of a separate black chart in 1965 and 1969. These black consumers were not unthinking, malleable sponges, who, racial loyalties notwithstanding, bought Motown products they did not really much like simply because Berry Gordy told them to, or because they were force-fed them on the radio. They bought Motown records because they could dance to them and relate to their timeless, witty, erudite and passionate messages of love, loss, loneliness, joy and belonging.

Moreover, black acts at Motown and elsewhere had always worn their sharp mohair suits and silk gowns with, as Marvin Gaye might have said, much pride and joy, seeing them as symbols of how far they had come from humble beginnings. Certainly, the spangled pursuit of success carried no stigma among black fans who had routinely been denied equal opportunity to compete for the financial rewards of the mainstream, but who in the 1960s glimpsed the prospect of a real change in their fortunes. While Gleason and other critics may have preferred their black artists poor and marginalized, Motown made the earnest bid for mainstream success and respect a matter of black pride.

Singer Kim Weston believed that it was the voracious black appetite for such conspicuous images of material success which explained much of Motown's extra-musical appeal and cultural resonance. "When I was coming up in Detroit I had no one to look up to who had made it. Through Motown's help and guidance, today's kids have all the Motown stars to emulate. We were from all sorts of backgrounds and we found success right here in our hometown". Fortunately, this fitted perfectly with Gordy's personal ambitions and his own conception of the role and responsibilities of black capitalists. For Gordy, the creation of personal wealth and the spirited pursuit of mainstream success was in itself a form of political, black economic and cultural leadership.

What Motown offered in its 1960s pomp, then, was less a dilution of some authentic black soul than a brash new urbane synthesis of pop, r&b and gospel, derived from, and perfectly fitted for, a particular moment in black and American history. Stylistically, Motown resolved some of the earlier musical and personal dilemmas of the black pop era, when a Jackie Wilson, or even a Sam Cooke, had sometimes struggled to reconcile roused black pride with the enduring dream of making it, the bigger the better, in the mainstream of American entertainment.

Realizing that dream was a large part of what the Movement was all about in the 1960s, and Berry Gordy succeeded better than any black man of his day. Between 1960 and 1969, Motown released 535 singles, of which 357 made either the Rhythm and Blues and/or pop charts. Of those records, 21 reached number one on both the pop and Rhythm and Blues listings; 6 made the top slot in the pop charts alone; 29 reached number one in the Rhythm and Blues charts only. By 1965, Motown had a gloss income of around $8 million and was the nation's leading seller of singles. Five years later it was the richest enterprise in African-American history. All this was achieved with a music which was fuelled by gospel and much closer to the "black" end of a national black-white musical spectrum than any popular style which had previously enjoyed such sustained and massive white appeal.

The British Invasion Transforms American Rock and Roll

David P. Szatmary

On February 7, 1964, four young men from England forever changed American music and popular culture. When the Beatles landed in New York, no one was quite prepared for the massive effect they would have on the adolescent generation after a mere nine-day stay in the United States. It was obvious that American youths were hungry for something new and exciting by mid-decade, and the Beatles not only satisfied this hunger but left the American kids wanting more. The subsequent British Invasion of the 1960s saw other English bands follow the Beatles' lead and bring an adulterated form of rock and roll back to its place of birth.

David P. Szatmary gives an account of this musical movement in the following excerpt from his social history of rock and roll. According to Szatmary, young musicians in the United Kingdom became extremely enamored with American rhythm and blues, which American GIs had brought to England during the Second World War. They blended this style with English folk music and created a new sound, the Mersey Beat. After the Beatles first carried this sound across the Atlantic, American teens grabbed hold of the danceable beat and the clean-cut image of most of

■

its purveyors. Taken with the whole package, legions of fans as well as young musicians imitated the look, the attitude, and the music of the British Invasion.

Subsequent British invaders like the Rolling Stones brought a more blues-heavy sound in their music, and their image was less dapper and more sexually charged than that of the Beatles. These bands also conquered America—not with the Mersey Beat but with the Chicago blues, a driving force behind rock and roll that ironically was overlooked in its native land. As Szatmary notes, only when American teens became charmed by the Stones and other British blues artists did they go back to investigate the American blues artists who had inspired the invaders, bringing the music full circle.

David P. Szatmary writes musical reviews and often contributes to the *All Music Guides* to rock, jazz, and blues. He currently resides in Seattle where he serves as the acting vice provost at the University of Washington.

FRIDAY, FEBRUARY 7, 1964, AT THE KENNEDY INternational Airport, New York, New York. Outside, a mass of screaming teenagers covered the rooftop on one of the airport wings. The crowd, mostly pubescent girls, had been waiting for more than eight hours in the frosty winter air. They considered themselves lucky: only those with special passes had been permitted on the roof, patrolled by dozens of uniformed security police.

Inside the terminal, huddled around the gate that admitted incoming passengers from London, more than 9,000 teenage girls, adorned with bouffant hairdos, oversized jewelry, and their mothers' makeup, shoved, clawed, and pushed each other in a mad attempt to get to the arrival entrance. They were separated from their goal only by a thin white nylon rope and a few airport guards. As the minutes passed slowly and the intensity mounted, the crowd was comforted by a voice from a transistor radio: "It is now 6:30 A.M. Beatle time. They left London 30 minutes ago. They're out over the Atlantic Ocean heading for New York. The temperature is 32 Beatle degrees."

Four of the passengers on Pan American flight 101 felt uneasy. "We did all feel a bit sick," remembered one. "Going to the States was a big step. People said just because we were popular in Britain, why should we be there?" Asked another: "America's got everything, George, so why should they want us?" A third: "I was worrying about my hair as well. I'd washed it, but when it had dried, it had gone up a bit." The fourth, the oldest and the leader of the group, sat silent and motionless in his seat.

As the plane neared its destination, a few wild screams from the airport broke the tense silence. Then an entire chorus of cries from girls on the rooftop alerted the crowd inside of the group's arrival. In a few moments, the frenzied wails of pent-up teenage passion sent tremors throughout Kennedy International Airport, increasing at a deafening rate. The girls started to half chant, half sing, "We love you Beatles, oh yes we do."

A Hectic Arrival

The plane landed safely and reached the hangar. Scurrying attendants pushed a platform toward the jet, the door swung open, and passengers started to descend the steps. Employees of Capitol Records shoved Beatle kits complete with wigs, autographed photos, and a button with the message "I Like the Beatles" at them. At last, four young Englishmen, who sported buttoned-down, Edwardian suits from Pierre Cardin and mushroom-shaped haircuts, walked out. After almost 150 years, the British had again invaded the United States. This time they would emerge as the victors. The Beatles had arrived in America.

The four lads from Liverpool—John, Paul, George, and Ringo—dashed toward a chauffeured airport limousine. They leapt in the car, locked the doors, and rode toward the terminal, assaulted by hundreds of girls who hurled themselves at the slow-moving automobile, clinging to the hood, the roof, and the sides. As they inched away, the foursome saw, pressed against the windows, the contorted faces of teenage fans who tried to catch a glimpse of their heroes before they were pulled away by other admirers.

The foursome broke loose from the crowd and headed toward the airport complex. After a short press conference, the

Beatles jumped back into the limousine and sped down the Van Wyck Expressway, reaching Manhattan about an hour and a half later. Though swarmed by hundreds of fans when the car stopped at New York's plush Plaza Hotel, the Beatles managed to pry the doors open and somehow make it into the hotel lobby, where they were escorted to a twelfth-floor room. There they discovered three screaming girls in the bathtub and called maid service for help. Throughout the night and for the next few days, the Beatles were protected by armed guards from ingenious girls who climbed the fire escapes and from conspiring groups of teens who checked in at the hotel, using the names of their well-to-do parents to penetrate the twelfth floor. Outside, the boys heard fans keep a twenty-four-hour vigil by chanting, "We want the Beatles, we want the Beatles."

Into American Living Rooms

On Sunday night, the new idols from across the Atlantic came into full view. Late in 1963, Ed Sullivan, the square-faced, stocky show business impresario, had witnessed a near riot at the London airport, where more than 15,000 screaming fans descended upon the terminal, delaying the Queen and Prime Minister Sir Alec Douglas-Home in order to welcome the Beatles back from a trip abroad. Impressed, Sullivan told the *New York Times*, "I made up my mind that this was the same sort of mass hit hysteria that had characterized the Elvis Presley days." He hurriedly located Brian Epstein, the dapper, brilliant manager of the group, and for less than $20,000 booked the Beatles for three appearances on his show.

On February 9, 1964, Sullivan showcased the Beatles. Seven hundred twenty-eight wild teenagers packed into the studio from which the *Ed Sullivan Show* was broadcast. They had battled 50,000 others for tickets to the show that featured the Beatles. When Sullivan introduced the foursome—"and now, the Beeeatles!"—the room erupted. Girls with checkered skirts and Macy blouses let out primal screams and pulled their hair, thrusting themselves toward the front of the stage or leaning perilously over the balcony. Some simply fainted. Few noticed that one of the microphones had gone dead. All eyes fastened on Paul, bobbing back and forth as he played a left-handed bass guitar; Ringo, smiling as he brushed the drumskins; John, yelling the lyrics over the din; and a rather dour, flu-stricken George, the youngest, skinniest member of the group, just looking down at the neck of his lead guitar. The screaming intensified. Explained one girl in the crowd: "You really do believe they can see you and just you alone, when they're up on stage. That's why you scream, so they'll notice you. I always felt John could see me. It was like a dream. Just me and John together and no one else." The show, ending amidst the wails, had been extremely successful. It had been witnessed by more than 73 million people across the country, more than 60 percent of all television viewers. . . .

Beatlemania

By the time the Beatles left New York for London on February 16, the entire nation had become aware of Beatlemania. Headlines in the staid *Billboard* told the story: "The U.S. Rocks and Reels from Beatles Invasion"; "Chicago Flips Wig, Beatles and Otherwise"; "New York City Crawling with Beatlemania"; and "Beatle Binge in Los Angeles." In the nine days during the Beatles' brief visit, Americans had bought more than 2 million Beatles records and more than $2.5 million worth of Beatles-related goods. They purchased blue-and-white Beatles hats; Beatles T-shirts and beach shirts; Beatles tight-fitting pants; Beatles pajamas and three-button tennis shirts; Beatles cookies; Beatles egg cups; Beatles rings, pendants, and bracelets; a pink plastic Beatles guitar with pictures of the four lads stamped on it; a plethora of Beatles dolls, including inflatable figurines, 6-inch-tall hard rubber likenesses, painted wood dolls that bobbed their heads when moved, and a cake decoration in the form of the Beatles. Others snapped up Beatles nightshirts, countless Beatles publications, Beatles ice cream sandwiches covered with a foil Beatles wrapper, Beatles soft drinks, and Beatles wigs, which Lowell Toy Company churned out at the rate of 15,000 a day. Selteab (Beatles spelled backwards), the American arm of the Beatles manufacturing company even planned for a Beatles motor scooter and a Beatles car. . . .

Some adults disapproved of the new rage. After the *Sullivan* show, the *Herald Tribune* called the Beatles "75% publicity, 20% haircut, and 5% lilting lament." To the *Daily News*, "the Presleyan gyrations and caterwauling were but lukewarm dandelion tea compared to the 100-proof elixir served up by the Beatles." Disregarding his personal ban on Sunday television viewing, evangelist Billy Graham watched the Beatles on *The Ed Sullivan Show* and believed that the performance revealed "all the symptoms of the uncertainty of the times and the confusion about us." Ray Block, orchestra leader on the *Sullivan* program, prophesied that the band "wouldn't last longer than a year," and actor Noel Coward said, "I've met them. Delightful lads. Absolutely no talent." Concert critic Louis Biancolli summed up the adverse reaction to the Beatles: "Their effect is like mass hypnosis followed by mass nightmare. I never heard anything like what went around me. I've read about the bacchantes and corybantes in wild Greek rites screaming insensately. They were antique squares compared to these teenage maenads."

Most media commentators, however, welcomed the clean-cut, well-tailored Beatles and their aristocratic manager. *Time* wrote that "the boys are the very spirit of good clean fun. They look like shaggy Peter Pans, with their mushroom haircuts and high white shirt collars, and onstage they clown around endlessly." The 1964 *Yearbook of World Book Encyclopedia* singled out the Beatles' "rambunctious and irreverent sense of fun" and the *Yearbook of Collier's Encyclopedia* likened the foursome to "Little Lord Fauntleroys."

Newsweek probably best captured the majority opinion when it labeled the Beatles "a band of evangelists. And the gospel is fun. They shout, they stomp, they jump for joy, and their audiences respond in a way that makes an old-time revival meeting seem like a wake. . . . The Beatles appeal to the positive, not negative. They give kids a chance to let off steam and adults a chance to let off disapproval. They have even evolved a peculiar sort of sexless appeal: cute and safe. The most they ask is: 'I Want to Hold Your Hand.'" The fun-loving Beatles seemed a perfect antidote to the pessimism that had engulfed America after John F. Kennedy's death a few months earlier. . . .

The intensity and magnitude of Beatlemania in America can be attributed, at least in part, to the postwar baby boom. In 1964, millions of pubescent and prepubescent Beatlemaniacs were part of the more than 43 million youths who had been born between 1947 and 1957. They searched for an identity and collectively latched onto the Beatles as a symbol of unity. As one Beatles fan told a reporter as she stood vigil in 1964 outside of a hotel where her heroes resided, "I'm here because everyone else is here." Though youths had idolized Elvis Presley, the mass hysteria of Beatlemania could only have occurred during the mid-1960s, when the majority of baby boomers were old enough to become interested in music. "We were just the spokesmen for a generation," explained Paul McCartney.

The Mersey Beat

In the mid-1960s, the Beatles, who had conquered the American music market by appealing to the baby-boom generation, paved the way for other British groups, some of them linked to Brian Epstein. "The biggest thing the Beatles did was to open the American market to all British artists," contended British promoter Arthur Howes, who planned the early Beatles' tours of England. "Nobody had ever been able to get in before the Beatles. They alone did it. I had brought over lots of American stars, but nobody had gone over there." By February 1969, *Variety* told its readers, "Britannia ruled the airwaves." "The advent of the [Beatles] now has shattered the steady, day-to-day domination of made-in-America music here and abroad." During 1964, British rock bands sold more than $76 million worth of records in the United States.

Some of the British groups had grown up with the Beatles in Liverpool. Gerry Marsden, a truck-driver who was a neighbor of the Beatles, in 1959 formed a band called the Pacemakers. Under the watchful eye of manager Brian Epstein, who signed the group in June 1962, Gerry and the Pacemakers established a following at the Cavern Club in Liverpool, frequently playing on the same bill as the Beatles. In 1963, they climbed to the top of the British charts with a song written for the Beatles, "How Do You Do It?" and followed with the chart-toppers, "I Like It" and "You'll Never Walk Alone," ending the successful year with an appearance on the British television show *Saturday Night at the London Palladium*. In May 1964, Gerry and the Pacemakers debuted in America on *The Ed Sullivan Show*, which helped promote the group's bestselling U.S. single, "Don't Let the Sun Catch You Crying."

They capped their career in 1965 by starring in the movie *Ferry Across the Mersey*, with a hit single of the same name.

Members of another Epstein act, Billy J. Kramer and the Dakotas, rose from their working-class backgrounds to stardom. Billy J. Kramer (a.k.a. William Ashton), a worker for the British Railways, originally sang with a group called the Coasters, but teamed with a Manchester combo, the Dakotas, on the advice of Epstein who signed the Liverpudlian in late 1962. Observed *The Big Beat*, an English fanzine: "The marriage of the zing singing of Billy J. to the true-beat accompaniment of the Daks has proven a brilliant stroke on the part of Epstein. These boys just have to step onto the stage and the fans go wild!". . . .

Along with the Beatles, these Liverpool groups delivered the "Mersey sound." Alexis Korner, a British blues innovator, found that "there was a certain brashness about the Liverpool music, which stamped it almost immediately—they played it the way they speak English, you know! You could definitely tell a Liverpool group. The Mersey sound was basically a guitar sound: lead guitar, rhythm guitar, bass guitar, and drums was the basic Liverpool setup.". . .

The British Blues Invasion

English groups playing American electric blues formed a flank of the British invasion. The British fascination with American blues started with Chris Barber's band. When the British Musicians Union ended the ban on American musicians in 1956, Barber and his bandmates began to invite American blues performers to England. "Chris Barber and I had started to bring American musicians to play with our band," remembered Harold Pendelton. "Muddy Waters came out on stage [in 1958] and played an electric guitar. This was the first electric guitar anyone in Britain had ever seen.". . .

Alexis Korner and Cyril Davies, two members of the Chris Barber band, helped popularize American blues among British youths. "Alexis and Cyril Davies were the only ones really playing blues in London at that time," remembered Rolling Stones drummer Charlie Watts, who originally played with Korner and Davies. "Cyril was a great harmonica player; he made a couple of very good records—'Country Line Special' was one. He and Alexis got together while Alexis was playing with Chris Barber, who had one of the biggest trad bands." By 1962, the two formed Blues Incorporated and landed a regular Saturday night job at the Ealing Club, which attracted youths such as Keith Richards, Mick Jagger, and Brian Jones, who occasionally performed with Korner and Davies.

As the Rolling Stones, Richards and his companions would take Chicago blues to youths like themselves on both sides of the Atlantic. "The Stones were [not] the first people into the blues in England, Alexis Korner and Cyril Davies were, but the Stones were the first ones who were young, you know," recalled Giorgio Gomelsky, the first manager of the Stones. . . .

The material chosen by the early Stones indicated their Chicago blues orientation. For their first single, recorded in March 1963, they covered Chuck Berry's "Come On" and Muddy Waters' "I Wanna Be Loved." Their first American album, *England's Newest Hitmakers*, included Slim Harpo's "I'm a Kingbee," "Carol" by Chuck Berry Willie Dixon's "I Just Wanna Make Love to You," and Jimmy Reed's "Honest I Do." Subsequent albums exposed teenage record buyers to R&B classics such as "You Can't Catch Me" and "Talkin' About You" (Chuck Berry), "Little Red Rooster" (Willie Dixon), "Mona" (Bo Diddley), and "Look What You've Done" (Muddy Waters). The Stones recorded many of these cuts at the Chess studio in Chicago. "Chuck Berry wandered in while we were recording 'Down the Road Apiece,'" a wide-eyed Bill Wyman told a reporter from *New Musical Express*, "and he said to us: 'Wow, you guys are really getting it on.' Muddy Waters was also there." Even the name of the band—the Rolling Stones—came from a tune penned by Muddy Waters, and in April 1963, the *Record Mirror* characterized the Stones as "genuine R and B. As the trad scene gradually subsides, promoters of all kinds of teen-beat entertainments heave a long sigh of relief that they have found something to take its place. It's rhythm and blues . . . and at the Station Hotel, Kew Road, the hip kids throw themselves around to the new jungle music like they never did in the more restrained days of trad. And the combo they writhe and twist to is called the Rolling Stones.". . .

The Stones conquered America on their second tour, which began on October 23, 1964, and featured a spot on *The Ed Sullivan Show*. During the 1950s and 1960s, Ed Sullivan provided the means for teens across the United States to hear rock-and-roll. He had helped promote Elvis Presley, had fostered Beatlemania, and had provided the springboard for British invasion groups such as Gerry and the Pacemakers, the Searchers, and the Dave Clark Five. "The power of the man [Sullivan] and his show was unbelievable," enthused Dave Clark, who appeared on the show seventeen times. "He was responsible for the success of the British invasion.". . .

The Blues Onslaught

Other British bands, enamored with Chicago blues, gained the allegiance of British and American teens. The Yardbirds were convinced of the power of the blues by the Rolling Stones. Around 1963, singer Keith Relf and drummer Jim McCarty "went to see the Rolling Stones because they started playing in Richmond, which was quite near . . . and we gradually listened to more of this R&B stuff, got more records," recollected McCarty. That year, McCarty's band, which included guitarists Chris Dreja and Top Topham, merged with Relf and bassist Paul Samwell-Smith, both of whom wanted to play more R&B like Jimmy Reed, Howlin' Wolf, and Chuck Berry."

The Yardbirds first performed as a backup band for Cyril Davies, and in 1963, replaced the Rolling Stones as the house band at the Crawdaddy club, owned by the first manager of the Stones, Giorgio Gomelsky. They debuted on record with a cover of Chicago bluesman Billy Boy Arnold's "I Wish You Would" and first charted with Don & Bob's R&B standard, "Good Morning Little School Girl." On a December 1963 tour of England, booked by Gomelsky, the band backed Sonny Boy Williamson. "A lot of the basis of our act was rearranged rhythm and blues," commented Dreja.

The Yardbirds featured a series of guitar wizards steeped in the blues. When lead guitarist Top Topham left for college in 1963, the band hired blues purist Eric Clapton, who "grew up loving black music." Clapton left the group in 1965 when he felt that the hit "For Your Love" sounded too pop. "I went back to Skip James and Robert Johnson—I spent years in that field and then I came back to the city blues, worked around there for a while, and I guess that's where my heart really still is," explained the guitarist.

After the departure of Clapton, the Yardbirds added the more rockabilly-influenced Jeff Beck. "We still played the blues—Jeff could play a great blues—but at the same time we were always looking to something new, something fresh," remarked McCarty. In 1966, Jimmy Page, who would later help invent heavy metal with Led Zeppelin, joined the group. By 1968, when they disbanded, the Yardbirds had scored blues-inspired hits in Britain and America with "I'm a Man," "Heart Full of Soul," "Shapes of Things," and "Over Under Sideways Down."

From the Muswell Hill region of London, a northern working-class suburb, came the Kinks. The band was formed in 1963 by R&B enthusiasts Ray and Dave Davies, Peter Quaife, and Mick Avory, who had briefly played with the Rolling Stones. In 1964, they unsuccessfully debuted with Little Richard's "Long Tall Sally." By September of the same year, the group topped the charts with "You Really Got Me," which almost defined power-chord rock. Dave Davies explained to *Melody Maker* that the distinctive sound originated because at that time "I was never a very good guitarist . . . so I used to experiment with sounds. I had a very small amplifier which distorted badly." The Kinks followed with the crunching "You Really Got Me" and "All Day and All of the Night" before turning toward a softer, music-hall style. Although charting in America, the group met disaster when U.S. authorities instituted a four-year ban on them for unprofessional conduct after their first American tour in June 1965. . . .

The British blues invasion of America provided notoriety for some blues pioneers. "We still have mostly Negro adults at our gigs," remarked B.B. King in 1966, "but I've noticed in the last year or so I've had a lot [more] of the white kids come than ever before." Muddy Waters noticed the same trend: "The Rolling Stones came out named after my song, you know, and recorded 'Just Make Love to Me' and the next thing I knew [white youths] were out there. And that's how people in the States really got to know who Muddy Waters was." In the mid-1960s, the sound of Chicago blues ironically had been introduced to American youths by British bands.

Jazz as an Expression of Black Nationalism

Michael J. Budds

Like rock and roll, jazz music has never been a singular entity. Jazz artists are influenced and inspired by innovations in music as well as by events in society at large. In the 1960s, an era marked by protest and experimentation, jazz musicians often dabbled in both. According to professor Michael J. Budds, one force that guided some black jazz players in the 1960s was the evolving social identity of African Americans as reflected in the stridency of the civil rights movement and the rise of black nationalism.

In the following selection, Budds describes how some black musicians of the decade felt compelled to use their music to speak out against traditional racism and give voice to the new black consciousness that struggled for what Budds calls "social, economic, and psychological independence." Following such disciples as the black Muslim leader Malcolm X, who demanded that African Americans seize what had been denied them, many black jazz musicians showed their allegiance to the radical, militant stance by creating music that was equally radical and often unharmonious. Drummer Max Roach, bass player Charles Mingus, and saxophonists John Coltrane and Archie Shepp are but a few of the jazzmen who Budds claims addressed the changing political climate in their 1960s recordings. These men experimented with new

■

Michael J. Budds, *Jazz in the Sixties: The Expansion of Musical Resources and Techniques.* Iowa City: University of Iowa Press, 1990. Copyright © 1990 by the University of Iowa. All rights reserved. Reproduced by permission.

sounds and new musical scales, according to Budds, to capture that sense of change and to communicate their support for it.

Michael J. Budds is a professor in the University of Missouri's School of Music. He has written several books on American and British music.

FOR MANY BLACK MUSICIANS DURING THE SIX-ties the act of playing jazz became a meaningful testimonial, a sincere form of protest and defiance that was, at the same time, personal, social, and artistic. Although the human feel-ings motivating such behavior did not originate with this gen-eration of performers, such expression through jazz repre-sented a conscious break with the past, a notable departure from tradition.

Black musicians have always been understood as a special symbol of the black American identity: their music has always been perceived as a light illuminating the black experience in America. This was the case in spite of widespread exploitation of black musicians by the mainstream entertainment industry and in spite of the general pattern of imitation by white musi-cians. In his history of black music in America, [poet Amiri] Baraka describes the relationship between music and the black experience as fundamental:

> I think it is not fantastic to say that only in music has there been any significant Negro contribution to *formal* American culture. . . . Only Negro music, because, perhaps, it drew its strength and beauty out of the depths of the black man's soul, and because to a large extent its traditions could be carried on by the "lowest classes" of Negroes, has been able to survive the constant and willful dilutions of the black middle class and the persistent call to oblivion made by the mainstream of the society.

For all practical purposes, the structure of the jazz world that had evolved in the United States up until that time may be de-scribed by the analogy of an imperialistic power and its colony. With minor exceptions, whites controlled the economic inter-ests: the night clubs, the booking agencies, the recording companies, the radio stations, the festivals, and the jazz periodicals. The critics, who exerted untold influence, were also in most cases white. Although individual whites who worked in this empire, especially the musicians, were often sincerely sympathetic to the black cause, the apparent segregation of management and worker made black musicians likely candidates for some form of activism. Their point of view, as expressed by Archie Shepp, was, "You own the music and we make it."

Making Claims on Jazz

Many jazz artists, accordingly, participated in the forefront of the movement for Black Nationalism. Angry young black musicians tended to accept and espouse a number of specific, highly controversial conclusions concerning the nature of jazz and its history. The following manifesto was considered in the pages of *down beat* magazine in 1966:

1. Only Negroes can play great jazz.

2. All the originators in jazz, the truly creative jazzmen—the innovators—were and are Negroes.

3. Jazz is Negro protest music that only Negroes and a few whites infused with something of a "black" outlook can understand and appreciate.

4. All Negroes in jazz have been, and are now being, exploited by whites and the "white power structure."

Such an interpretation of historical fact and contemporary problems along racial lines was unquestionably and, perhaps intentionally, self-serving. The times required that the subject be treated in a sensational, propaganda-like manner. With some qualification, a factual basis for these assertions exists, but such an intolerant explanation also contributes to a distortion of history. In retrospect, the extreme nature of these "battle cries" suggests a form of deliberate overcompensation—as if the time-honored tradition of injustice could only be rectified by shocking tactics.

The eloquent, if intentionally menacing, writings of saxophonist and playwright Archie Shepp indicate the tenor of the rhetoric of militant black jazz musicians:

The Negro musician is a reflection of the Negro people as a social phenomenon. His purpose ought to be to liberate America aesthetically and socially from its inhumanity. The inhumanity of the white American to the black American, as well as the inhumanity of the white American to the white American, is not basic to America and can be exorcised. I think the Negro people through the force of their struggles are the only hope of saving America, the political or cultural America.

Cultural America is a backward country; Americans are backward. But jazz is American reality—total reality. . . . Some whites seem to think they have a right to jazz. Perhaps, that's true, but they should feel thankful for jazz. It has been a gift that the Negro has given, but [whites] can't accept that—there are too many problems involved with the social and historical relationship of the two peoples. It makes it difficult for them to accept jazz and the Negro as its true innovator.

Jazz in the service of Black Nationalism effected a dramatic means of expressing social doctrines and the emotional disposition of its adherents. Nurtured on the examples of Charles Mingus, Max Roach, John Coltrane, and Archie Shepp, a generation of outspoken black jazz musicians emerged and made its mark [according to poet Amiri Baraka] by "using . . . music as an eloquent vehicle for a consciousness of self in America."

Jazz as Social Protest

This attitude—this insistence on the extra-musical meaning in jazz—and the awareness that it represented something new in black music can be documented by numerous performances from the period. In the liner notes to an especially important collection of avant-garde performances entitled *The New Wave in Jazz* (Impulse A–90, 1965), Steve Young provides an introduction that cites both the anger and the hope played into the improvisations:

Here then is the music of a new breed of musicians. We might call them "The Beautiful Warriors" or witch doctors and ju ju men . . . astro-scientists, and magicians of the soul. When they play they perform an exorcism on the soul, the mind. If you're not ready for the lands of Dada-Surreal à la Harlem, South Philly and dark Georgia nights after sundown, night-time Mau Mau attacks, shadowy figures out of flying saucers and music of the spheres, you might not survive the experience of listening to John Coltrane, Archie Shepp or Albert Ayler. These men are dangerous and someday they may murder, send the weaker hearts and corrupt consciences leaping through windows or screaming through their destroyed dream worlds. But this music, even though it speaks of horrible and frightening things, speaks at the same time so perfectly about the heart and to the heart. This music, at the same time it contains pain and anger and hope, contains a vision of a better world yet beyond the present and is some of the most beautiful ever to come out of men's souls or out of that form of expression called Jazz.

This album, recorded at a benefit concert for the short-lived Black Arts Repertory Theatre/School, which Baraka directed, features Coltrane, Ayler, Shepp, trombonist Grachan Moncur, and trumpet player Charles Tolliver.

Many other examples in which jazz was assigned the task of social protest can be cited. In a passage from the liner notes for the album *Extensions* (Blue Note LA006G, 1970), pianist McCoy Tyner summarizes his philosophy of music-making at that time: "Music tells a story—it may summarize the past or redirect the future. Compositions written and played by Black musicians are vehicles to express the struggles and sufferings of Black people." In this instance the listener was also provided with a description of the emotional and pictorial topic of each piece on the album. Tyner, a Black Muslim, also supplied quotations from the Koran, the Moslem book of fifth containing the revelations of Mohammed.

Saxophonist John Coltrane produced one of the most poignant examples of program music and protest music in jazz with "Alabama" (*Live at Birdland*, Impulse AS–50, 1963), a haunting modal elegy for the four child victims of a racist's bomb at a church in Birmingham in 1963. The piece presents a sequence of moods: sorrow, resignation, defiance, and hope. This musical prayer is a striking illustration of jazz as a form of "oral history," as the piece immortalizes a particular incident in American history. Details of the music, moreover, were reportedly determined by the speech rhythms of Martin Luther King's eulogy for the slain children. The rhythm of the word "Alabama" (long-long-short-long) can be heard in a phrase that recurs several times as the piece unfolds.

Shepp's Frustration

The music of Archie Shepp exhibits many dynamic examples of the union of jazz and contemporary black concerns. Two of his recorded performances, for example, serve as musical memorials to black victims and are labelled as such. Racist violence in the form of a lynching is the theme of a powerful 1964 performance entitled "Rufus (Swung, his face to the wind, then his neck snapped)" on *Four for Trane* (Impulse AS–71, 1964). The following year Shepp responded to the assassination of Malcolm X with the elegy "Malcolm, Malcolm—Semper Malcolm" from the recording *Fire Music* (Impulse AS–86, 1965). According to Nat Hentoff, the composition "is meant to symbolize the various elements in Malcolm's life and spirit, and in the life and spirit of this country's black people.". . .

With Shepp himself delivering the brief poem as the music commences, the performance becomes part eulogy, part lamentation, and part expression of hope. The music was borrowed from an unfinished work by Shepp intended to pay tribute to another assassinated black leader, Medgar Evers, who was murdered in 1963.

On the same album is found "Los Olvidados" (The Forgotten Ones), which relates to Shepp's work as a counselor and music teacher in Mobilization for Youth, a federally-sponsored program for underprivileged children on the Lower East Side of New York City. Here the message addresses both the good intentions of the saxophonist and the greater struggle to enrich the lives of children in a project that was doomed because of inadequate resources and an ineffectual bureaucracy. The theme of the music, according to Shepp, is "the frustrations of that gig—knowing I couldn't do anything meaningful about that scene." The name for this work was borrowed from the title of a 1950 Mexican film directed by Luis Buñuel and shown in the United States as *The Young and the Damned*.

Black Nationalist musicians purposefully sought a music that would provide them with an identity that could not be absorbed by the white musical world. They accomplished this in part by being "free." The term not only implied freedom to experiment with new techniques, but more important psychologically, freedom from the musical trappings of Western society—most notably, the popular song, the tempered scale and harmonic system of European music, and the metric straitjacket of middle-class American popular music. Likewise, the militancy of their social views found a parallel in the rigid meaning they assigned to their music in general. In the words of Archie Shepp, jazz is

> one of the most meaningful social, esthetical contributions to America. . . . It is antiwar; it is opposed to Vietnam; it is for Cuba; it is for the liberation of all people. . . . Why is that so? Because jazz is a music itself born out of oppression, born out of the enslavement of my people.

Because music had been the notable endeavor in which black Americans had been permitted freedom of expression, these black musicians perceived their efforts in this new environment of racial politics as a continuation and a confirmation of that freedom: "Music not only must bring esthetic, but also social order into our lives."

A Message Too Exclusive

In spite of the inflamed pronouncements that accompanied the music of the Black Nationalists, their musical practice was not as exclusive as its proponents would have, perhaps, preferred. Some of their experiments were similar in nature to those conducted by other progressive musicians who acknowledged no association with this socio-religious movement. The fact that Black Nationalists gave their music special meaning or believed that their music communicated their social agenda was a product of the times and its idealism.

Because of its highly experimental nature, its exhausting intensity, and its extra-musical content, the "protest music" of Black Nationalist jazz musicians was rarely able to attract a large portion of the jazz audience. The historical importance of these endeavors, however, must not be minimized by commercial considerations. It is important as well to emphasize that the protest movement in jazz gained currency among black musi-

cians of all ages. Numerous recorded performances by musicians of the preceding generation, most notably drummer Max
Roach and bass player Charles Mingus, also exhibit a similar
commitment to the black cause and its expression in jazz. In
such cases, the musical language often differed from that established by the avant-garde.

Woodstock Symbolizes the Promise and Failure of the Counterculture

Bruce Pollock

The Woodstock music festival, which took place in
August 1969 at a farm in upstate New York, has gone
down in the annals of history as one of the largest
gatherings of like-minded individuals. Attendance estimates for the three-day event reach as high as
250,000. All of these devotees came to watch some of
the biggest names in rock-and-roll music—such as
Jimi Hendrix, the Jefferson Airplane, and the Who—
perform in a single venue. Through rain, mud, and
heat, the crowds remained peaceful and attuned to
the music and its inspired sense of brotherhood. For
many who were at Woodstock, and many others who
would claim they were there, the concert would come
to symbolize the collective harmony of the 1960s
generation.

Not everyone who was at Woodstock, however,
retains such a rosy view of the event. In the following
article, music historian Bruce Pollock records the tes-
timony of John Sebastian, a founding member of the
Lovin' Spoonful and a guest at the Woodstock festival. Sebastian recalls how he was asked to perform on

■

Bruce Pollock, *When the Music Mattered: Rock in the 1960s.* New York: Henry Holt and
Company, 1983. Copyright © 1983 by Bruce Pollock. Reproduced by permission.

the Woodstock stage to fill time between two booked acts. He complied willingly, and thus saw the event from both on and off stage. Sebastian claims that, while the festival was successful in the sense that so many people were able to function together harmoniously in the span of three days, it may have ultimately been a failure because that spirit was not carried on in later years. Sebastian argues that Woodstock was more or less a collective of stoned seekers who had made it to the end of the decade but had yet to find the rewards promised by hippie idealism. Instead, as Sebastian notes, the counterculture trappings were quickly picked up by marketers who commoditized the spirit into salable products. And for its part, the youth movement lost its momentum and was soon gobbled up by the very cultural forces it was opposing.

Bruce Pollock has written articles for *Playboy*, *Musician*, and the *Village Voice*. He is also the author of *Hipper than Our Kids: A Rock & Roll Journal of the Baby Boom Generation* and *When the Music Mattered: Rock in the 1960s*, from which this selection is taken.

MANY IN THE THRONGS THAT COLLECTED AT the Woodstock Festival in August 1969 undoubtedly were lured there by the rumors of an appearance by Bob Dylan. Woodstock, after all, was where the legend had lived in hiding since his disastrous motorcycle accident of 1966. At Woodstock, it was promised, Dylan would stage his return to live performing, his poetry restored, his energy and charisma resurrected to take on the challenges of the repressive seventies looming just over the rise. Instead, it was Dylan's absence that rock fans had to deal with, as he, like many another sixties figure, chose to abdicate his role as savior of the country. But in his absence his titles left a message that is obvious: "Tears of Rage," "Nothing Was Delivered," "I Shall Be Released," "You Ain't Goin' Nowhere," "Too Much of Nothing."

It may be unfair to caption Woodstock "Too Much of Nothing," but the image and the reality of the event are not at all difficult to separate. To the general public and posterity it was presented as nothing less than a victory celebration, something akin to the founding of a city in the state of bliss. But this ritual rain dance was a mudbath, a financial disaster. The bands in attendance, though awed, were ultimately removed from

To many who attended the August 1969 rock music festival, Woodstock represented the culmination of the hippie movement.

their musical moment. There were just too many people, too much rain, too little planning. A sloppy good time, for sure, but more discomfiting than euphoric, except in retrospect.

A walk-on at Woodstock, singularly at one with the event (he claims he was tripping), John Sebastian uniquely blends both the up side and the down side of the sixties musical experience, of which Woodstock was the culmination. . . .

Expectation Unfulfilled

The legend on the poster they sell to tourists at the Woodstock general store reads: "Let Woodstock be a shining example." Although the rock festival that put the town on the culture map . . . actually took place in nearby Bethel, the example of Woodstock is still hailed whenever shock troops from the abortive rock revolution gather together to mourn the pipe dreams of those halcyon days when the music was churning and burning and rock 'n' roll seemed capable, all by itself, of great and impossible things: love, peace, equality, acid in the drinking water.

But Woodstock is a symbol nonetheless for the enormous expectations, exalted sense of history, and agonized, messy downfall of a generation caught up in the momentum of its own power over events. Those who had dislodged Lyndon Johnson thought for sure that they could change the world through force of will and an electric guitar, endless theoretical conversations, and a little stamping of the feet. But as high as it got on those smoky nights, it never got high enough to withstand the pull of gravity—the crunch of repression.

By the time the troops got to Woodstock—to offer to the media and the world, out of the mud and music, humanity, heat, rain, bad acid, and faulty plumbing, a smiling, eight-by-ten glossy album-cover photo and documentary film still—the revolution was effectively over. The civil rights movement and the peace movement had gone down with Bobby Kennedy and Martin Luther King, Jr. [California governor] Ronald Reagan had clamped a lid on Berkeley protest. The great society had turned to mush. The blissful borders of an acidhead Nirvana had been invaded by Charles Manson and the Weathermen [an underground terrorist organization of radical leftists]. Having believed in the magic of rock 'n' roll, having opened

themselves up through sexual exploration and chemical experimentation, street theater and political activism, the Woodstock constituency was faced with the prospect that it all may
have been an illusion.

In their disappointment at being deserted by all things
countercultural, some would drift to self-destruction, some
would look to reincarnation, others would take it out on the
music. But at Woodstock, for three days, this vast and tattered
and freaky graduating class could sit within the shadow of the
Big Rock Candy Mountain one last time before contemplating
the long journey outward alone.

John Sebastian, the Hippie Representative

If anyone could have represented Woodstock to its constituency, it was a performer whose image was in tune with the
multicolored, evanescent joviality of that famous lawn party
for half a million of the faithful: John Sebastian, founder of the
Lovin' Spoonful and coiner of the phrase "the magic of rock
'n' roll," a man of a thousand T-shirts. In the documentary
film of the festival, Sebastian is seen onstage unshaven, in a
flowered jacket, outrageously delirious at appearing to such a
historic throng.

"I was basically on about a triple acid trip right when they
asked me to play," Sebastian explained. "Which answers the
question: Can a man play his own songs when he couldn't find
his car?" He was at Woodstock as a guest, manning a backstage
tent and relaxing in typical fashion. "I was not scheduled to
perform," he said. "I was enjoying being off that particular series of days, so I accepted an awful lot of acid from Wavy
Gravy, who kept saying 'You know, these kids are really having
bad trips, but it's not that bad.' . . .

Usually Mr. Control, the essence of bedspectacled post-
Beatles hip, Sebastian, as recorded for posterity by the cameras
of Woodstock, oozed ecstasy, congratulating the audience for
its inescapable righteousness. In voicing such heady palaver,
Sebastian was no doubt echoing the sentiments of everyone
wedged in there on Max Yasgur's grazing grounds. "Still, in
retrospect I was very unhappy about the impression I gave
people at Woodstock." Sebastian told me. . . .

"I think I play and sing a lot better than I played and sang that day," he continued. "I was sort of one with the experience of Woodstock, I guess, so that stood me in some sort of short-term good stead, but in the long run I'm sorry that the highest visibility performance I've ever given was one where I was smashed beyond belief."

Sharing the mixed emotions of most who were there, Sebastian saw Woodstock as the culmination of the decade's frantic momentum. "We were coming out of an unpopular war, where people had a rallying point," he said. "They'd had a lot of practice in various civil rights and antiwar demonstrations at being part of large numbers of stoned people, somewhat in disarray, but able to keep it together." As high as Woodstock was, as a moment and a symbol, its aftermath was depressing and depressingly American.

"No sooner was there a Woodstock than there were a million natural-yogurt companies cropping up," Sebastian remarked. "I think we are devourers of our own culture and cannibalized a lot of things that could have happened out of Woodstock. A media culture can absorb and regurgitate stuff so fast that it loses meaning almost before it's out of the pot. Somehow every mood that was created was suddenly turned into a marketable item. I regret that more of the spirit that existed at that point in time could not carry over to the sort of cocaine-and-glitter thing that filled the void once it was gone. But I guess those, are the jokes.". . .

The Specter of Death

The era of great parties [that characterized the 1960s] dwindled into a sloppy series of financial and musical baths, poorly planned and atavistic festivals, celebrations, love-ins, and human carnivals through the early years of the seventies, which all attempted to exploit Woodstock vibes. Merely a year after Woodstock, in fact, two of its producers, Michael Lang and Artie Kornfeld, were suing the other two, John Roberts and Joel Rosenman, for ten million dollars. Rapidly, that pure and innocent body language, rock 'n' roll, began to take itself as seriously as its sidewalk critics did, becoming in the process something more and something less. When *Hair*, the first major rock musical-opera, moved uptown to Broadway in 1968, the die was cast. Following its success musicians and groups with theatrical and classical and poetic pretensions abounded, performing to a chorus of impassioned critical rhetoric. Trying to be all things to all people, rock 'n' roll got lost in its flamboyant gestures. . . .

"The rock stars became the cowboys," Sebastian reflected. "The generation before, it had been either you were a singer or you were tough. Then Elvis Presley made it okay to be tough and sensitive. Then the Beatles made it okay to be cute and tough and sensitive. So it was just mounting permission to be more and more for musicians, until it was possible to be Hopalong Cassidy."

But Hopalong Cassidy rode off into the sunset, and so many other cowboys traded in their cap pistols for three-piece suits. Hank Williams, Jr., said it in a recent country song, "All My Rowdy Friends Have Settled Down."

"For my generation," John Sebastian said, "it would be more like 'All My Rowdy Friends Have Died.' None of the guys I considered rowdy ever stopped—and they all died." Among sixties freaks and faithful, their names are almost clichés now, our honored dead: [Jimi] Hendrix, [Janis] Joplin, [Jim] Morrison. The assassination of John Lennon. In Sebastian's circle alone there was Cass Elliot, Michael Bloomfield, Lowell George, Tim Hardin. "I'd say Timmy knew exactly what he was doing and lived, to my mind, about twenty years longer than I ever expected," Sebastian said. He felt much the same way about [bluesman] Lightnin' Hopkins, who died in 1982, nearing the age of seventy. "Knowing his habits from 1965, I was frankly just awed that he lasted so long. The man would wake up and have breakfast of two eggs and a jelly glass full of gin. But he never seemed to get sloppy drunk.". . .

You couldn't bring back the sixties without releasing once again that chill of imminent death, not only to rowdy friends and superstars but to assorted street fighters and draftees, acid casualties and living zombies, and otherwise normal neighbors caught in the crossfire of events, who strayed too close to the edge. It's why the rest of us are sometimes thought of as survivors.

4

EXAMINING POP CULTURE

The Influence of the 1960s on Post-60s Pop Culture

Idealism in Post-60s Rock Music

David P. Szatmary

One legacy of the 1960s is its music. In the following article, David P. Szatmary explains how the ethos of 1960s music influenced the music of subsequent artists. Beginning in the 1980s, bands and artists such as U2, REM, Tracy Chapman, and the Indigo Girls kept the spirit of the former decade alive not only in their respective musical attitudes and styles, but also in their role as activists for humanitarian causes. According to Szatmary, these artists' use of celebrity to bring light to political injustices and to raise money and awareness in combating poverty and other social ills reveals an inherited belief that music can be a powerful force for social change.

Szatmary also discusses the advent of the compact disc in the 1980s as contributing to renewed interest in the music of earlier decades. Compact discs resurrected many artists of the 1960s and made their music available to both consumers and radio stations. In fact, it was the latter's creation of "classic rock" playlists that helped bring 1960s music to a new audience, ensuring its survival and marketability ever after.

David P. Szatmary is a music critic and a contributor to the *All Music Guides* to rock, jazz, and blues. Currently, he is acting vice provost at the University of Washington in Seattle.

■

David P. Szatmary, *Rockin' in Time: A Social History of Rock-and-Roll, 5th Edition.* Upper Saddle River, NJ: Prentice-Hall, 2000. Copyright © 2000 by Pearson Education. All rights reserved. Reproduced by permission.

THE RETURN TO 1960s' IDEALS OCCURRED around mid-decade, when the economy started to decline and the social order became increasingly stratified. In 1981 and 1982, after nearly three decades of prosperity in the United States, economic conditions began to worsen as unemployment increased to almost 10 percent. Though expanding at an encouraging 8 percent annual growth rate in the first half of 1984, the U.S. economy again began to falter later in the year. Wage gains slowed, unemployment stood at nearly 8 percent, and personal consumption declined. "The economy," noted one analyst in early 1985, "appeared to be teetering on the brink of a recession, having swung from boom to bust conditions in one quarter."

Economic stratification added to concerns. While finding an increase in the number of families that earned more than $50,000 a year, a Census Bureau study in 1984 reported that nearly 66 million Americans in 36 million households received government benefits in the third quarter of 1983. Of the total, which represented nearly 30 percent of the U.S. population, about 42 million Americans received food stamps, welfare, subsidized housing, or Medicaid.

Many baby boomers who expected the prosperity of their youth especially felt the effects of the recession. "When we grew up in the '50s and '60s, we were told the world would be our oyster," explained Richard Hokenson, a forty-six-year-old demographer in New York City. "Now life's turned out to be more of a struggle than we were told it would be." In 1984, *U.S. News & World Report* referred to the baby boomers as "the disillusioned generation, people in their 20s and early 30s who wonder whatever happened to the American dream.". . .

The Benefits

Benefit concerts such as Band Aid and Live Aid . . . demonstrated a reawakened interest in improving the world. Started after singer Bob Geldof of the Boomtown Rats saw a report on the Ethiopian famine, Band Aid united a number of English musicians who recorded the song "Do They Know It's Christmas?" which was featured at an Ethiopian Benefit Concert at the Royal Albert Hall in December 1984 and sold 3 million copies. Live Aid, also conceived by Geldof to aid the starving masses in Africa, involved a 16-hour concert on July 13, 1985, simultaneously televised from Wembley Stadium in London and JFK Stadium in Philadelphia. It boasted 1960s' rockers such as Eric Clapton, Mick Jagger, Neil Young, Pete Townshend, and Paul McCartney. "This concert is the ultimate expression the pop industry can make," stated Bob Geldof. It was watched by more than 1.5 million people, and raised more than $120 million in cash and goods, most of which helped alleviate the situation of famine victims. "I think Live Aid and Band Aid were the beginning of an awareness," observed Jackson Browne, the 1970s' singer/songwriter who helped organize the MUSE [Musicians United for Safe Energy, "No Nukes"] benefit.

Other rock-and-rollers, most from the 1960s, organized benefits. The Grateful Dead, having played countless free concerts during their heyday, organized a benefit to protect the world's rain forests. "It's a problem we must address if we wish to have a planet that's capable of supporting life," said the Dead's Bob Weir. Peter Gabriel, formerly of Genesis, which had fashioned a theatrical folk-based English rock, united with Bruce Springsteen to tour in support of Amnesty International, which sought to free political prisoners around the world. Springsteen, who donated more than $200,000 to the charity, told one sellout crowd on the tour, "The great challenge of adulthood is holding on to your idealism after you lose your innocence."

Steve Van Zandt, nicknamed Little Steven, organized rock and rollers against racism in South Africa. In late 1985, after leaving the E Street Band for a solo career, he established Artists United Against Apartheid, an organization that lashed out against the brutal discrimination toward blacks in South Africa, particularly the $90 million, white-only Bophuthatswana resort, Sun City, which had hosted Rod Stewart, Linda Ronstadt, and Queen. Little Steven planned an album, a book, and a video to combat apartheid, enlisting the support of sixties rock stars such as Springsteen, Pete Townshend, Ringo Starr, Bob Dylan, Keith Richards, and Lou Reed. Taking the civil rights movement into the international arena, Little Steven donated nearly a half-million dollars to causes supporting the anti-apartheid struggle.

The anti-apartheid furor among rock musicians peaked

with Paul Simon's *Graceland*. After participating in USA for Africa, in late 1984 the former folk rocker traveled to South Africa to record with South African musicians. "To go over and play Sun City, it would be exactly like going over to do a concert in Nazi Germany at the height of the Holocaust," Simon reasoned. "But what I did was go over and essentially play to the Jews." He hoped the record, featuring the South African choir Ladysmith Black Mambazo, would serve as a "powerful form of politics" that would attract people "to the music, and once they hear what's going on within it, they'd say, 'What? They're doing that to these people.'" In 1985, *Graceland* topped the British chart and climbed to the number-3 slot in the United States.

Children of the Sixties

The renewed interest in social causes shaped a number of new bands, notably U2. Formed in Dublin by schoolmates Bono (Paul Hewson), The Edge (David Evans), Adam Clayton, and Larry Mullen Jr., the band won a talent contest sponsored by Guinness beer in March 1978. After two years of local gigs, it released the debut single "11 O'Clock Tick Tock" which failed to chart. The group recorded two albums, *Boy* (1980) and *October* (1981), which attracted critical attention but sold few copies.

U2 began to infuse its music with a political message. In October 1982, during a concert in Belfast, Northern Ireland, Bono introduced the song "Sunday Bloody Sunday," which detailed the historic political troubles in Ireland. A few months later, the band released *War*, combining rock with various strands of punk. "Punk had died" recalled The Edge. "We couldn't believe it had happened, and *War* was designed as a knuckle buster in the face of the new pop." The guitarist continued: "We loved the Clash's attitude early on and Richard Hell and the Voidoids, the [Sex] Pistols. We wanted love and anger. We wanted a protest record, but a positive protest record." Symbolizing U2's connection to a 1960s'-type protest, in July 1984 Bono sang a duet with Bob Dylan on "Blowing in the Wind" at a Dylan concert in Ireland.

The band continued to demonstrate its commitment to the 1960s ideals. Though beginning to replace hard-driving guitars with more ethereal, echo-laden sounds engineered by producer Brian Eno, U2 dedicated its 1989 hit "Pride (In the Name of Love)," to Martin Luther King Jr. It contributed to Band Aid, played in the Live Aid spectacular in Wembley Stadium, appeared on the anti-Sun City project, and performed on Amnesty International's twenty-fifth anniversary tour. In 1986, the band raised funds for the unemployed and performed in San Francisco for another Amnesty International benefit. By the next year, when it hit the top of the charts with *Joshua Tree*, U2 had become spokesmen for change. As Bono remarked in 1987, "In the '80s, which is a barren era, we look back at the '60s as a great reservoir of talent, of high ideals, and of the will and desire to change things." As with his counterparts in the 1960s, the singer was interested in "a revolution of love. I believe that if you want to start a revolution you better start a revolution in your own home and your own way of relating to the men and women around you."

Midnight Oil, an Australian band formed in 1976 when Jim Moginie, Rob Hirst, and Martin Rotsey of the hippie band Farm teamed with law student and singer Peter Garrett, applied 1960s' ideals to its own country. "I grew up loving people like John Fogerty," remembered drummer Hirst, "people who commented on what America was going through during the Vietnam War. It was rather natural that this band would choose to comment on the country that it knows better than anywhere else." In their first two LPs, the band decried the nuclear arms race and the dominant presence of U.S. military forces in Australia. In *Diesel and Dust* (1986), which sold 3 million copies and reached the Top 25 on both sides of the Atlantic, they protested white Australian oppression of the indigenous aborigines, touring the back country to demonstrate their support of aboriginal attempts to regain traditional lands. With *Blue Sky Mining* (1990), Midnight Oil told the tale of Wittenoon miners who contracted asbestos-induced cancer on the job during the 1950s and 1960s and who first secured redress from mine operators in 1988. "What Midnight Oil does have is an underlying belief in the human spirit," remarked Peter Garrett, who in 1984 ran for the upper house of the Australian Parliament on the Nuclear Disarmament Party ticket and served as the president of the Australian Conservation Foundation.

The 1960s' spirit also inspired a late 1980s folk boom led

by Tracy Chapman. Born to a poor family in Cleveland, Chapman had always been interested in social issues. "As a child," she told *Rolling Stone*, "I always had a sense of social conditions and political situations. I think it had to do with the fact that my mother was always discussing things with my sister and me—also because I read a lot." While at Tufts University in Medford, Massachusetts, she began performing on the Boston folk club circuit.

One day in 1986, while playing at a Boston coffeehouse called the Cappuccino, Chapman met fellow Tufts student Brian Koppelman, who introduced the protest singer to his father Charles, the head of the largest independent music publishing firm in the world. Within a few months, with the help of the elder Koppelman, she landed a contract at Elektra Records and secured as her manager Elliot Roberts, Bob Dylan's manager. "You don't have to be a genius to see that words are coming back in a large way, that there's more social consciousness in people, and the apathy that there was for years seems to be slowly declining," observed Roberts in late 1988. That year, Chapman released her first, self-named album, which hit the top of the chart; the next year she followed with the Top-10 *Crossroads*. "She has grasped the threads of misery and dissent of *these* times, sewn them together deftly, and delivered them unforgettably," remarked folkster Joan Baez.

Other female folk singers sang to injustice. A veteran of the Greenwich Village folk scene, Suzanne Vega combined the New York influences of Bob Dylan and Lou Reed to produce the hit "Luka" (1987), a song decrying child abuse. Other folksters such as the Indigo Girls [Amy Ray and Emily Sailer] lobbied for Amnesty International, Hand Gun Control, Voters for Choice, the Coalition for the Homeless, and indigenous people. "We work with a lot of activists," explained Ray, "and it has mostly to do with disenfranchised communities, or with issues that have come about because of the corporate structure of the United States."

R.E.M. delivered a socially conscious message through a brand of jangly, folksy rock. Formed in 1980 by vocalist Michael Stipe, guitarist Peter Buck, bassist Mike Mills, and drummer Bill Berry, the group perfected a Byrdsian guitar-driven sound. After four albums that garnered a cult following, in 1987 the band hit the Top 10 with *R.E.M. No. 5: Document* and followed with *Green* (1988), which urged listeners to protect the environment. R.E.M. lobbied for Greenpeace, voter registration, and liberal political candidates. "In the late 80s, I was influenced and politicized to the point that I felt like I wanted to try to make some of these things [songs] topical," remembered Michael Stipe.

Classic Rock and the Compact Disc

A return to 1960s-style protest, coupled with the advent of the compact disc, led to a nostalgic rebirth of 1960s rock. "Speaking of the '60s artists," *Billboard* informed its readers in a wrap-up of the decade, "one of the more notable trends of the late '80s was the commercial success of many bands that made their commercial debut more than 20 years ago." "And, as the fairy tales say, it seemed that it might be time again for legends," added *Time* in late 1989. "Twenty years later, there was suddenly on every side the familiar sound of the '60s."

Radio helped promote 1960s' rock. Largely ignoring the TV generation, which preferred the rapid-fire video bites of MTV, it programmed oldies for the baby boomers, who still purchased the greatest number of records and served as the prime target of most advertisers. In 1988, of the roughly 10,000 stations in the country, more than 500 radio stations broadcast oldies exclusively. The next year, contended Ken Barnes, editor of the trade magazine *Radio and Records*, at least 40 percent of all radio programming fell into the "classic rock" or "oldies" categories. In early 1990, oldies station WCBS-FM grabbed the number-1 spot in the New York market. Radio, observed CBS Records president Al Teller, seemed to be "chasing the yuppie generation to its grave."

Along with oldies radio, the compact disc helped revive an interest in classic rock and rescued a troubled music industry. Introduced to the mass market in late 1982, it provided record buyers with a high-quality, digital, durable, long-lasting format. The compact disc, commonly called the CD, contained millions of digitally encoded pits, which held musical information that could be converted into almost noise-free sound through a low-powered laser beam. Less than 5 inches in diameter, the polycarbonate plastic disc only warped at temperatures over 220 degrees Fahrenheit, could not easily be scratched like a vinyl record, and produced up to 75 minutes of music with a dynamic range of 90 decibels.

The silver platter quickly became more popular than its vinyl counterpart. During its first two years on the market, the CD appealed primarily to jazz and classical music fans, who appreciated the expanded dynamic range. As the price of compact disc players plummeted from about $900 in 1983 to less than $150 in 1987, and as the cost of a compact disc declined from $18 to $14 during the same period, the convenient CD began to sell to the rock record buyer. In 1985, 16.4 million CDs were purchased worldwide. Three years later, more than 390 million compact discs were sold internationally to account for sales of more than $6 billion, compared to 295 million vinyl LPs sold for $2.8 billion. Cassette tapes, becoming the most popular format for music during the late 1970s and registering even greater sales after the introduction of the portable Walkman cassette player in 1981, outperformed both with sales of more than $6.7 billion for 787 million units sold. However, in late 1990, the CD even began to outsell the cassette in retail outlets such as Tower Records.

At the end of the decade, many industry executives predicted the demise of the vinyl LP. "I assume the death knell has been sounded, and there's not much we can do about it," mused Joe Smith, president of Capitol Music–EMI. "It's gasping for breath," agreed Russ Solomon, founder and president of the Tower Records chain. "We'd like to hold on, but unfortunately the world is not going that way." "Our little flat friend the record is what drove the business for a long time, but we're going to be out of the business," mentioned Bob Sherwood, senior vice president of Columbia Records.

Depictions of the 1960s in Film and Television of the 1980s

Daniel Marcus

In the following excerpt from his book on the resonance of the 1950s and 1960s in later decades, Daniel
Marcus examines the way in which movies and television of the 1980s dealt with the legacies of the 1960s.
According to Marcus, some baby boomer directors
made films that showed how 1960s survivors struggled to hold on to their idealism in the world of
1980s corporate capitalism. Others depicted characters who had either sold out their hippie values of
peace and brotherhood to yuppie materialism or at
least struggled to find a way to live in both worlds.

Turning to television, Marcus examines some of
the most popular programs like *Family Ties*, which
portrayed a generational conflict between the parents, who clung to a hippie ethos, and their son, who
extolled the virtues of Reagan-era economics and the
advantages of greed. The author also takes note of
the desire in such shows as *The Wonder Years* to re-
press the political demons of the decade in favor of
indulging in wistful nostalgia for lost innocence.

Daniel Marcus teaches media arts and studies in
the Department of Communication at Wayne State
University in Detroit.

■

Daniel Marcus, *Happy Days and Wonder Years: The Fifties and the Sixties in Contemporary Cultural Politics*. New Brunswick, NJ: Rutgers University Press, 2004. Copyright
© 2004 by Daniel Marcus. All rights reserved. Reproduced by permission.

IN ADDITION TO REVISITING THE PUBLIC EVENTS of the 1960s, films and television programs also traced the distance between the values and expectations of the period and the purported realities of Baby Boomer life in the 1980s. In dramas and comedies of regret, nostalgia, and bewilderment, the 1960s were represented as a time of youthful idealism, extravagant if vague expectations, and exciting cultural progress. These energies were shown to be fading by the 1980s, replaced by a baleful, hard-won maturity.

Lost Values

The first film to explicitly explore this dynamic was John Sayles's *The Return of the Secaucus 7*, which announced the arrival of the new independent American cinema in 1981. Manifestly low-budget and from a discernedly left-wing perspective, the film dramatized the disillusionment and modest hopes of Sixties activists facing uncertain futures at the dawn of the Reagan era. The film's themes and structure were echoed two years later in *The Big Chill*, a major-studio release produced by former 1960s media activist Michael Shamberg. In *The Big Chill*, the past political activities of seven friends who reunite for a friend's funeral remain vague, but their occupational changes are carefully drawn to be emblematic of the shift from public-mindedness to private materialism—a public defender has become a real estate lawyer, an inner-city teacher has turned to celebrity journalism, a psychologist has descended to drug dependence and dealing. Their deceased friend was never able to accommodate the turning away from Sixties values, and had become a lost soul before killing himself.

The group expresses regret at the diminution of their dreams and the clouding of their original, unifying purposes. The happiest of the survivors, however, is also the most conservative, a small businessman prospering in the Reagan era and impatient with Sixties political and social nostalgia (while steadfastly refusing to allow new additions to his Sixties record collection). The film was alternately hailed as an authentic voice of the historical experience of the Baby Boom generation and criticized as a whiny, half-hearted yuppie (before the label was popularized) tract. It helped to solidify the notion that the Sixties generation had become sell-outs, and that those wanting to live according to Sixties ideals had faded into social and cultural obsolescence.

The Big Chill's combination of Boomer upward mobility and nostalgic regret was brought to television by *thirtysomething*, which inspired a similarly mixed critical response. The central couple in the series' circle of middle-class friends and relatives are Michael and Hope, who continually evaluate and compare their present domesticated, corporate lives with their earlier artistic and feminist ambitions. The paths not taken are represented by Melissa, a single woman and photographer, who is beset by neuroses about her romantic and work life, and Gary, a politically rebellious but immature academic. The series' most famous episode mimics the old *Dick Van Dyke Show*, as Michael tries to make sense of his life by measuring it against the domestic ideal represented by the model 1960s television family. The series' dramatic development shows Michael and Hope growing into acceptance of their roles within a traditional, middle-class nuclear family, even as Michael is first tempted by, but ultimately becomes disillusioned with, cut-throat corporate politics. In perhaps the only strong protest seen on American entertainment programming against government policy during the Persian Gulf War, he quits his job in advertising in a fit of residual dovish disgust at the rampant jingoism around him. . . .

Reversing the Dynamic

The popular film and television depictions of the Sixties legacy feature privileged professionals muddling through with varying, degrees of acceptance to present social circumstances. . . . [But] one television series enjoyed huge popularity by comically mining the contrasts between Sixties values and contemporary conservatism. *Family Ties* split the warring impulses between the Sixties and the Reagan Eighties generationally, as two liberal parents contend with their Reagan-loving teenage son, in a reversal of the generational dynamic of *All in the Family* and other post-Sixties productions. In *Family Ties*, it is Sixties-based attitudes of antimaterialism, social concern for the disadvantaged, and open-mindedness toward others that are imbued with an aura of steady maturity, through the portrayal of the family's upper-middle-class parents, an architect

The Commercial Failure of 1960s Nostalgia

Marketing the 1950s and 1960s to the baby boomers was a phenomenon that began in the late 1970s and carried through the next decade. As writer and editor Landon Y. Jones attests, the reception of this manufactured nostalgia has been varied. While boomers look back fondly on the 1950s, they have not wholeheartedly embraced the repackaged 1960s.

The baby boom's nostalgia almost exclusively involves the fifties and first few years of the sixties. But what about the rest of that difficult decade? Shouldn't it be a potential wellspring of nostalgia, too? After all, the largest number of baby boomers spent their formative years in the sixties. Feelings for those times seemingly ought to be more intense than for the fifties and ought to evoke an even lustier nostalgic boom.

It didn't happen. Attempts to merchandise the sixties in movies like *Sergeant Pepper's Lonely Hearts Club Band* and *I Want to Hold Your Hand* flopped. The television version of *Loose Change* failed, too. Yet the promoters persisted. In 1979, a group tried to cash in on what looked like a sure-fire success: a tenth anniversary concert at Woodstock. The name, as they pointed out, was practically a brand name. There would be a movie, and a sound-track album, and spin-off paperbacks, T-shirts, and maybe lunch-boxes. A computer would distribute tickets nationwide at $75 a

and a public television programmer. The series' comic energy, however, stems from Michael J. Fox's portrayal of their son Alex as a greedy, know-it-all Reagan youth; as impetuous and immature as Alex is, he seemingly has time and determination on his side in his battle against the mild Sixties homilies of his parents. Perhaps that is why Ronald Reagan claimed it as his favorite show on television. . . .

The films *The Flamingo Kid* (1984) and *Dirty Dancing*

pop. It was a perfect idea in every respect except one. Nobody cared. This is what one musician said to the *Washington Post* when he heard of the project.

> Look what the establishment did to the fifties. They took whatever was relevant to us and turned it into a million-dollar cliché. Everybody thinks it was like *Grease* and *Happy Days*. Now they're getting ready to sell us the Sixties. Those were great times. Why can't they let our dreams alone?

On the commercial level, sixties nostalgia does not work. This is not surprising. The sixties have an altogether different place in the life of the baby boom than the fifties. Nostalgia for the fifties can satisfy the baby boom's need for wholeness and reassurance. But the sixties were schizophrenic; things were flying apart. Nostalgia exists to shore up personalities troubled by change, but the sixties offered no such solace. Indeed, the sixties are more likely to remind people of the disharmonies in their lives. The sequel of *American Graffiti* was predictably a failure. By updating the characters into the disorienting and disjointed sixties—complete with flower children, protests, raucous rock, and Vietnam—the filmmakers lost the connection that had made the original film so effective. *More American Graffiti* was truer to its period, too, which is why it failed. It no longer fulfilled the emotional needs of the audience.

Landon Y. Jones, *Great Expectations: America and the Baby Boom Generation.* New York: Coward, McCann & Geoghegan, 1980, pp. 247–48.

(1987) revisited the early 1960s, the years *American Graffiti* had defined as the last innocent period before the onslaughts of the later part of the decade. *The Flamingo Kid*, directed by *Happy Days*'[1] mogul Garry Marshall, keeps a light-hearted tone throughout, but *Dirty Dancing* offers hints of what is to come, as the heroine of its coming-of-age story becomes more

1. *Happy Days* was a TV series about the 1950s.

aware of the civil rights movement and other social concerns just as she awakens to her sexuality. . . . *Dirty Dancing* depicts a Sixties concern for social justice as another sign of innocent youth rebelling against uncaring adults. Once taken up, Sixties activism can function as an entry into adulthood and a maturity more enlightened than that of the previous generation's.

Every age is someone's Golden Age of childhood innocence. As late and post-Boomers reached adulthood and gained access to media production in the 1980s, the 1960s began to be reconfigured by those whose associations with the period were at variance with the usual identification of the late 1960s as an era of social chaos, political divisiveness, and widespread violence. *The Wonder Years*, created by producers born in the late 1950s, depicted the adolescent travails of its hero with a tone of rueful but appreciative nostalgia. The series does not ignore the public events of the time—the premiere episode takes place in the wake of Robert Kennedy's assassination and features a major character learning of her brother's death in Vietnam. The focus of the series, however, is on a fundamentally innocent exploration of teenage sexuality and romance, friendship, and personal ethics, taking place in a suburban environment so often identified with 1950s sitcoms like *Leave It to Beaver.*

The prime authority figure, however, is not the family's father, as in Fifties family comedies. Rather, the adult voice of the young hero serves as an ever-hovering narrator to explicate the meanings of his younger self's experiences. The vantage point of the present allows him to rewrite the 1960s from the perspective of a younger cohort of the Baby Boom generation, to define the era as a source of worthwhile personal values and familial coping skills. The success of *The Wonder Years* shows that the work of a younger group of cultural producers can provide complications to popular meanings of an era. The series provides a much more positive and somewhat less tendentious portrayal of the late 1960s than found in previous political or cultural discourse.

Woodstock '99: Three Days of Violence, Rape, and Commercialism

Christopher Caldwell

The Woodstock festival that took place in the summer of 1969—called a celebration of peace, love, and music—is a hallmark of the togetherness and jubilation that unified much of the youth culture of the sixties. To commemorate the event's thirtieth anniversary, promoters John Scher and Michael Lang (who were behind the original event) organized a three-day music festival featuring several popular contemporary performers. While their intention was to re-create the positive atmosphere that characterized the original event, the concert was stained by riotous behavior and crass commercialism. With alcohol fueling the revelry, concertgoers were responsible for at least four rapes, destructive bonfires, and the looting of a souvenir storage truck. Also, mud and feces were thrown at performers while they were onstage. In the following article, journalist Christopher Caldwell examines the 1999 festival and its significance.

Caldwell concludes that Woodstock '99 revealed that the members of the 1960s counterculture had become part of the mainstream. By charging inflated prices and showing little regard for concertgoers, the promoters made it clear that Woodstock '99 was a commercial venture, not a counterculture event.

■

Christopher Caldwell, "When in Rome . . . Woodstock, Again," *National Review*, August 30, 1999, p. 29. Copyright © 1999 by National Review, Inc. Reproduced by permission.

Thus the behavior of the young people who rioted was more consistent with the antiestablishment spirit of the 1960s than were the actions of the promoters.

Caldwell is the senior editor of the *Weekly Standard*, a conservative magazine.

THE SECOND COMMEMORATION OF WOODSTOCK, at the former Griffiss Air Force Base in Rome, N.Y., resulted in two rampages. Both of them had the Sixties chant of Peace-Love-and-Understanding as a pretext.

First, a frat-boy-saturated crowd groped—and perhaps raped—a number of the bare-breasted girls being passed over the mosh pit and, once the music had stopped, emptied a couple of 18-wheelers full of souvenirs and smashed a handful of automatic-teller machines. Second, Richard Cohen and other columnists keen to defend the "spirit" of the original Woodstock reaffirmed their willingness to achieve Peace-Love-and-Understanding, by force of arms if necessary. In tones that would make a drunken Serb plead on his knees for moderation, Cohen looked at a Wirephoto of teenagers looting a souvenir truck and announced: "I want these guys arrested. . . . I want everyone else in the picture arrested also."

In the rush to assign blame for the greatest incident of rock wilding since a dozen were stomped to death at a 1979 Who concert, the bands were first. Limp Bizkit, Rage Against the Machine, and (my compliments on the name) Insane Clown Posse were singled out early. Not wholly without reason. Rage Against the Machine ended its set on the eve of the riots with the novel send-off: "F*** you. I won't do what you tell me."

Counterculture Has Become Establishment

Here's where Cohen and his like are trying to have it both ways. One can be appalled at the mayhem that ensued, but still admit that it's hard to think of anything more in the spirit of the original Woodstock than Rage's taunt. The '69 concert, held at Max Yasgur's farm upstate, was defined not just by what it was for (Peace-Love-and-Understanding) but also by what it was against (Vietnam, conformity, and capitalist exploitation). But as the decades have passed, the "Woodstock Experience" has come to be—for most of its members—indistinguishable from the American Establishment Experience.

Evidence of the mellow way in which the former counter-culture has bled into an establishment culture comes from the loudly proclaimed disappointment of Woodstock '99 promoters John Scher and Michael Lang (who helped set up the original Woodstock) that the festival didn't end more quietly. "Concert officials had planned to end the show on a more reflective note," the *Boston Globe* reported. But Scher and Lang's idea of "a more reflective note" was Peter Gabriel's closing of the first Woodstock commemoration, five years ago [in 1994], with his ballad "Biko." The song is about anti-apartheid politician Steve Biko, killed in 1977 by South African special forces. To think that a song about a democracy activist murdered by an authoritarian regime is supposed to lull an audience to sleep indicates the quiescence that has settled on the counterculture between 1969 and now.

Michael Lang explained the riots by saying, "I don't think the kids were making an anti-Woodstock statement. I think it was an anti-establishment, anti-everything statement." What he missed was that, now, Woodstock is the establishment. Fifty-two-year-old Tom Fall of Putney, Vt., had been at the original Woodstock, and he relived old memories while working as a vendor at the 1999 one. He professed himself shocked at the turn events took. "This was supposed to be peace, love, and harmony," he said. But he was wrong, too. This was not about peace, love, and harmony. It was about making tons of dough for the Woodstock Generation by exploiting the Woodstock Generation's children.

A Capitalist Enterprise

But there was a political protest at Woodstock '99, and Don Waslelewski of Hudson, N.H., had no hesitation in proclaiming what it was about. "I blame Michael Lang," he said. "He totally overpriced everything. He forgot what Woodstock is all about. . . . It's 95 degrees outside and the guy is selling water for $5 a pop." This didn't cut much ice with such tribunes of the privileged class as Richard Cohen. "The economic justification given by some is just plain lame," he wrote. "If the Woodstockians thought the price of a hot dog was excessive ($5), they need not have bought one. If they thought $4 was too much to ask for a bottle of water, they are right. But these prices are in line with what's charged at standard rock concerts."

But Woodstock was not a standard rock concert. It involved holding kids incommunicado for several days at the height of a heat wave that killed hundreds up and down the east coast. Woodstock's promoters charged $10 for burritos and $12 for mini-pizzas, all of it going into Michael Lang's pocket. It wasn't just that water cost four and five dollars a bottle—it was that the concert promoters appear to have shut off the water in order to promote sales. And they didn't clean the toilets! The port-a-potty doors were wedged open all weekend by sloping hills of turds. "They were expected to live like animals but spend money like kings," is how the *New York Times* described the gripe of an angry 47-year-old Woodstock-nostalgic, standing there with her 2-year-old granddaughter.

"If I were a Woodstock promoter," says Cohen, "I would offer a reward for the names of the looters and I just might hire some bounty hunters to look for these kids." . . . What was Cohen after? Not the "spirit" of the Sixties generation, but the interests of the Sixties generation. Maybe he can't tell them apart. At Woodstock '69, he'd've backed the youngsters. At Woodstock '99, he backed the '69ers, now bloated plutocrats, who were ripping the youngsters off.

It's enough to make you want to smash capitalism. According to John Strausbaugh, the editor of the *New York Press* who was at the original Woodstock 30 years ago, "What's arrogant is that the promoters were trying to exploit the kids with their own nostalgia. When the kids rebel . . . well, they rebel. That's what kids are for! It's about time one of these 19-year-olds looked at us and said, 'Well . . . you started it!'"

FOR FURTHER RESEARCH

Books

Alexander Bloom, ed., *Long Time Gone: Sixties America Then and Now.* New York: Oxford University Press, 2001.
This anthology contains several essays on cultural as well as political aspects of the decade. Perhaps the most useful are the ones that examine life in the counterculture, the "living theater," and the homosexual subculture.

Peter Braunstein and Michael William Doyle, eds., *Imagine Nation: The American Counterculture of the 1960s and '70s.* New York: Routledge, 2002.
This collection of essays covers many facets of the counterculture. One chapter contends with the shaping of minority identities; others examine media, pop culture, and cultural politics.

Michael J. Budds, *Jazz in the Sixties: The Expansion of Musical Resources and Techniques.* Iowa City: University of Iowa Press, 1990.
Much of Budds's research explicates the changes in technical style and therefore will likely appeal to experienced musicians. But the latter half of this book discusses jazz in its social and artistic contexts and reveals, for example, the connection between jazz and poetry, religion, and politics in the 1960s.

Gerald Early, *One Nation Under a Groove: Motown and American Culture.* Ann Arbor: University of Michigan Press, 2004.
Early's accessible prose makes this a good entry point into an examination of Motown and its cultural impact.

David Farber, ed., *The Sixties: From Memory to History.* Chapel Hill: University of North Carolina Press, 1994.
Ten essays are collected in this book. Each discusses some aspect of the 1960s, from the sexual revolution to America's pursuit of war in Vietnam.

Todd Gitlin, *Years of Hope, Days of Rage.* New York: Bantam, 1989.
Although Gitlin's focus is on the political evolution of the decade, he also explores the cultural and social aspects of the 1960s.

Van Gosse and Richard Moser, eds., *The World the Sixties Made: Politics and Culture in Recent America*. Philadelphia: Temple University Press, 2003.

This anthology of essays examines how the 1960s influenced the politics and social fabric of later decades. Specific pieces discuss the plight of Vietnam veterans, the political awareness of the gay community, and the legacy of the consumer culture.

Jay S. Harris, ed., *TV Guide: The First 25 Years*. New York: Simon & Schuster, 1978.

Although this work may be more difficult to find, it is an excellent resource for those interested in television's golden age. Harris compiles various articles culled from the pages of *TV Guide*, including fascinating pieces from the 1960s that reveal what reviewers thought of television programming at the time.

David E. James, *Allegories of Cinema: American Film in the Sixties*. Princeton, NJ: Princeton University Press, 1989.

In this book James considers mainly underground and experimental films, but his objective is to show the different kinds of film narratives that emerged in the 1960s. Although the book is fairly academic, novice film buffs can glean quite a bit of information from James's text.

Blanche Linden-Ward and Carol Hurd Green, *American Women in the 1960s: Changing the Future*. New York: Twayne, 1993.

A thorough study of women's changing roles and identities in the 1960s. Chapters discuss such topics as political activism, youth culture, education, dress, and work.

Marco Livingstone, *Pop Art: A Continuing History*. New York: Harry N. Abrams, 1990.

One of the better overviews of the pop-art world in the 1960s and beyond, Livingstone's work details individual artists and their motivations to create art that comments on consumer culture and questions modern values.

Daniel Marcus, *Happy Days and Wonder Years: The Fifties and the Sixties in Contemporary Cultural Politics*. New Brunswick, NJ: Rutgers University Press, 2004.

Marcus examines the impact of the 1950s and 1960s upon present-day politics and pop culture. He looks at such diverse topics as the birth of MTV and the election of President Bill Clinton and shows how they resulted from the power and legacy of the baby boom.

Arthur Marwick, *The Sixties: Cultural Revolution in Britain, France, Italy, and the United States, c. 1958–c. 1974.* Oxford, UK: Oxford University Press, 1998.
> Marwick, a British academic, discusses the cultural revolution of the 1960s as it was played out in four different countries. His analysis is always comprehensive and his insight into the changing culture of America is excellent.

Joan Morrison and Robert K. Morrison, *From Camelot to Kent State: The Sixties Experience in the Words of Those Who Lived It.* New York: Oxford University Press, 1987.
> This collection of firsthand reminiscences exemplifies how those who lived through the turbulent decade remember that time. Because these storytellers have the benefit of hindsight in describing the past events, their recollections are especially revealing.

Bruce Pollock, *Hipper than Our Kids: A Rock & Roll Journal of the Baby Boom Generation.* New York: Schirmer, 1993.
> Pollock's book deals with music from the 1950s to the 1990s. His four chapters on the bands of the 1960s discuss the social as well as musical dimension of their work.

Steven D. Stark, *Glued to the Set: The 60 Television Shows and Events That Made Us Who We Are Today.* New York: Free Press, 1997.
> Stark's book offers brief essays on sixty television programs and events that shaped American culture. Many of these are drawn from the 1960s and provide excellent analyses of pop culture as reflected on mainstream America's window to the world.

David P. Szatmary, *Rockin' in Time: A Social History of Rock-and-Roll.* Upper Saddle River, NJ: Prentice-Hall, 2000.
> This work covers rock and roll music from its birth through the 1990s. What makes the project appealing is that besides narrating the history of the music, it focuses on the social impact of rock. Chapters on the 1960s include discussions of surf music, Motown, acid rock, the British Invasion, teen pop, and folk music.

Barbara L. Tischler, ed., *Sights on the Sixties.* New Brunswick, NJ: Rutgers University Press, 1992.
> This anthology comprises several essays. Some focus on political and social upheaval, but others have a cultural bent. Especially attractive are the pieces that discuss the legacy of the 1960s.

Richie Unterberger, *Turn! Turn! Turn!: The '60s Folk-Rock Revolution*. San Francisco: Backbeat Books, 2002.
> In Unterberger's analysis, rock music was a powerful force for social change in the 1960s. From East Village folkies to the gathering at Woodstock, music of that decade found ways to combine protest with a beat and, in turn, brought the message of revolution to an entire generation.

Brian Ward, *Just My Soul Responding: Rhythm and Blues, Black Consciousness, and Race Relations*. Berkeley: University of California Press, 1998.
> Ward traces the history of rhythm and blues music through the lens of an expanding black consciousness in the 1950s, 1960s, and 1970s. His cultural focus makes this expansive work a good resource for learning about how the music contended with racism, capitalism, and black empowerment.

Web Sites

Everything60s.com, www.everything60s.com.
> This Web site compiles information mainly about the pop culture aspects of the decade. Music, fashion, and film are discussed in various articles and reminiscences. Interesting personal recollections from famous singers and other personalities from the 1960s are included.

The Fifties Web, www.fiftiesweb.com/fashion/cool-clothes.htm.
> These fashion pages are part of a larger Web site devoted to nostalgia and pop culture of previous decades. The sections on 1960s fashion detail clothing, makeup, and hairstyles of the decade. Text explains trends and innovations, and pictures illustrate the specific styles.

The Sixties Project, http://lists.village.virginia.edu/sixties.
> Originally put together by humanities scholars, this expansive Web project has grown to include input from many people who lived through the decade or have studied it academically. The site contains useful firsthand accounts from 1960s survivors, primary documents from the era, filmographies, and scholarly articles, among other unique exhibits.

INDEX